The Whisper Of Your Soul

A Guide Book for your Spiritual Journey of
Awakening, Discovery and Enlightenment

Karen Hackel

The Whisper Of Your Soul

A Guide Book for your Spiritual Journey of
Awakening, Discovery and Enlightenment

Karen Hackel

www.thewhisperofyoursoul.com

Copyright ©2010 Karen Hackel

ISBN- 1453760490
EAN-139781453760499

Cover art by Robyn Rosenbaum

Contents

Thank you to my Guides
for the beautiful writings
and messages

Introduction by Karen Hackel

I remember falling asleep when I was about six years old and feeling as though I was floating above my body and watching myself sleep. I clearly remember "floating" myself into the family room and observing my parents in the evenings. It seemed so natural to me. I would often have these visions of flying...

Years later, when my oldest sister Marian, was diagnosed with breast cancer at the age of 32, my father also began having visions. But his were visions of words that suddenly appeared to him without warning or preconception.

While skeptical of their origins, my father began channeling these beautiful flowing words of love and healing, recording them on paper and then sharing them with family and friends. We were all tremendously inspired by these continuous beautiful writings and anxiously awaited new writings for which he refused to take credit.

Sadly, my sister succumbed to breast cancer in 1989 at 36 years old. The words that flowed to my father during Marian's heroic battle abruptly ended when she died.

But from time to time, I would read his writings and ask him to write some more. He never wrote again.

The last message that my father received was from a Guide who claimed to be the Guide of my father's youngest daughter, Karen.

That person is me.

Ten years passed. During that time, I too was diagnosed with breast cancer at 35 years old, less than six months after our treasured son, Brett, was born. I went through surgery, aggressive chemotherapy and radiation - all the time feeling very positive and spiritual. I accepted the negative hurdle, feeling there was a force larger than me and healing would occur. I felt so connected to everything within me and around me. I confronted death and in a peaceful way experienced the fear of dying. Throughout this period, I was tremendously helped by keeping a journal chronicling my treatments and feelings.

In December 1998, without warning, my beloved father passed away. Our family's shock was compounded by geography. My father died in South Africa, where I was born and raised. But my surviving sister, Linda, and our families live in America.

Each day of the week following his passing, I was jolted out of bed at around 5:30 a.m. After a few days of these early morning awakenings, I was guided by an external force to take out a paper pad and pen, and start writing. Jumbled words initially came through, but they soon turned to beautiful poems.

Like my father's writings years before, these words were not my thoughts. I was a conduit... a messenger who simply wrote what I received.

I shared these words with friends and family members who were so comforted, they encouraged me to keep the connections open. So, I did.

And the messages continue to flow effortlessly through me. All I do is sit in silence, allow the writings to come forth in the stillness and write them down.

Many have asked how these writings come to me. I was dubious and skeptical, just like my father, when he began writing. I asked my Guides about the writings: Whose thoughts are these? How does this happen? How do I explain these writings? What is going on? How? Why?

The answer resonated clearly with these words:

Does it really matter

Your hand and pen are the vehicle

To share what the universe has to offer

You opened your mind

You opened your heart

And the sharing could begin

The thoughts come to you with clarity

There is no censorship

The less you think

The stronger the message to be relayed

Don't think

Just write

Don't second guess

What you feel you may write

There is no right or wrong

Only what you feel you hear

So write with free abandon

The less you think

The quicker the messages will come

They will flow freely

They will cascade like a waterfall

Each drop of the waterfall

Representing different thoughts

Different beliefs

Together the drops will come together

To form a beautiful waterfall

So it will be with your writings

Each lesson will be able to stand alone

But together the lessons will reveal

So much more

Coming together drop by drop

Lesson by lesson to create a waterfall

Illuminated by the sun

To create a kaleidoscope of colors

Like a rainbow

In all her magnificence

The colors will radiate

And shine through

To enjoy and experience

The splendor of it all

My writing ritual is to light a candle. I sit at a desk in a quiet room overlooking the woods. I am silent and breathe deeply. After a few minutes, I generally yawn a few times and it feels as though I am in a deeper state. I normally write a couple of sentences to alert my Guides that I am open and ready to receive messages. I sense what needs to be written - it is as though the words flow into my head and I write them down.

When I take the time, the messages come to me. But, life and living happen and months sometimes pass between writings. I strive to balance my time and energy. But being human, I don't center myself as often as desired to let the writings come forth. Since graduating college, I have worked full time in corporate, small business and not-for-profit environments. I started a promotional products company in 2007. Additionally for the past sixteen years, I have been deeply committed to volunteering for the Susan G. Komen Race for the Cure to raise awareness about breast cancer. I am also actively involved in my son's life and all his activities. So finding the time to write is a continual challenge I face. I take comfort in knowing that all is according to plan and I will find the time to write when the time is right.

I never erase or correct anything and all the writings are in their original state without any editing. After receiving the messages, I always thank the Guides. Generally, the writings take ten minutes to half an hour as the words flow quickly. The only structure is the initial capitalization of each line. Each segment carries a message of inspiration to which the reader can immediately connect.

Writings include elegant, easy-to-understand metaphors. Lack of punctuation allows the reader to pause as he or she wishes. Unlike usual discursive writing that forces the reader to engage one's mental capacities, this poetry – with its simple and direct approach - evokes feelings, remembrances and hope. The stanzas serve like the ending of a breath, encouraging the reader to contemplate what preceded before going forward.

These poems can be read aloud or silently. One will find new ideas and wisdom with each reading. The poems are meant to be savored like a cello concerto or sip of fine wine. They can be read again and again for deeper understanding because these writings tap into one's innermost truths, where the heart and soul meet the universal mind.

You may wish to use the white space around each stanza to write your own thoughts and insights. Be encouraged to rethink something in your life – heal an old hurt, ask for forgiveness, right a wrong, start a new project. You may gain a new perspective or have a new perception of an old paradigm. Regardless of how you use these writings, I hope you will feel calm and peaceful as you read. So read a passage or two before bed, or pick up the book and read a random segment when you feel unusual stress. Peruse a few pages to jumpstart your day. With every reading, you will be reinvigorated and inspired.

Many who have read these writings feel comforted. They were the ones who persisted and encouraged me to share these words of love and healing. It is through their persuasion that I finally took the time and effort to put these special writings into the book you now hold in your hands. I believe these writings are meant to be shared.

The messages follow in the order and format received. The only additions are that each has been given a title for easier reference and reading. Also at the end of some poems there are excerpts that I have added. I hope this book answers some of your questions and provides feelings of peace, love, comfort and healing. May it help guide you back to your true self, your essence, your core for it is a book about awakening and listening to *The Whisper Of Your Soul.*

I am grateful for this unique gift. I feel this incredible link – not only to my father, but to the connections he had through his writings. In essence, I am universally connected and so are you.

This book is my gift to you.
May you continue your
journey in light and love.

This Book is Comprised of
Guided Messages and Teachings

I am eternal love
I am your light
I am your flame
I am always with you

NO LIMITS

When all is grey around you
Look up to the sunshine
And see the brightness
I'll be there
When all is grey around
Remember I love you
With all my heart and soul
You are my guiding light
Together we walk
Together we run
Through pastures and meadows so green
Like kids with no troubles
Free
Home at last – free
Running, flying
No limits
Just beautiful
So at peace
Living so fully
Watching over you all
Loving, caring, hugging, touching
Helping you slow down
To learn
All part of life

I AM FREE AS A BIRD

The way is yours for the asking – the way is yours for the taking. The way is as it should be. Acceptance is a beginning. Understanding is the key to great love. You are all blessed and I am here for all of you. Like the blossoms on the tree I am there for you. In every sunrise and every sunset I am there. In the green trees and the blue sky I am all around. Open your eyes and I am always there. Time is just a fraction of your being and everything has a time. Give it all space – it is there. The leaves have fallen off the trees but the spring will come in all her splendor and you will all be healed. The sun and the moon they are there for you, the stars, the sky and the trees, just like I am here for you, forever. Watching and smiling and protecting you all the time. Just remember we are all together. It is paradise – so peaceful, so joyous, so special. But, I know there are tears for me and I understand, but everything is the way it should be. There is meaning to everything. First, there is the light, that glows eternally all around and you are all basking in my light. I will spread it over you all and the peace, strength and resolution will come. It is there for all of you – if you just look at all there is to see. So much abundance, so much love, so much energy – it is something that is so glorious. I am free as a bird, fast as a lion, large or small. I am everything. I am eternity. I am in everything. I am all around. So glorious – so at peace. I am light. There is no darkness here – only light and love.

WE ARE ONE

In life and in death – we are one. A bond never to be broken. Through this lifetime and other lifetimes we will be together. It is all a circle that keeps going round and round – for eternity. We will come and we will go – passing through different planes and dimensions but always the bond will be there. So many lessons to be learned, so many teachings to be taught – so much time. Here, there, everywhere – we are all learning and praying and growing. Reaching upwards and feeling the love and acceptance. It is within reach if you just slow down – open your heart and the love force is there, the peace and the answers. Open yourself up. The rainbow is love to you in her multi-colored splendor and you must see her beauty. But, so too is the lifeless tree beauty. Everything is energy and life and vibrant.

In life and in death – we are one.
A bond never to be broken

YOU ARE THE LIGHT

You are the light – feel yourself basking in the presence

It is all around, so bright, so full, so vital. It is all around

The love is there to sustain you and to send you higher

You are surrounded by light, by love, by beauty

Look around, it is everywhere

You see it with your eyes

You feel it with your senses

You know it is there

Open yourself up – let go and experience the light

It is there for you to experience always

The tears have been shed and the healing has begun

One piece at a time like a tall building, brick by brick by brick. All the pieces together in their own time. And so it is with life one layer at a time and then the next. The gentle unfolding of the layers will reveal so much to you and all around you. Step by step in your own time, at your own pace. There is no rush; there is so much time to experience the beauty

It is ever present, you are ever present

In the morning light and in the last rays of sunlight, it is there. Every moment, every day, every week. Never missing a beat

It is always there and yours for the asking

You are surrounded by light,
by love, by beauty

THE SPIDER WEB

The morning dawn is fading
As a new day breaks
A day full of potential
Endless possibilities
It is all there for you
To make the most
To grasp it
To live it
To experience it
Taste the moments
Explore the details
The day is just unfolding
So much to do
So much time
Time is limitless
Like a vast ocean
It goes on and on
Time is but a fraction
Of what you know it to be
The moment is all there is
Embrace it
Live it
Savor it
Each moment unfolds
Gently, peacefully, gradually
For you to experience
In its fullness
Its beauty

Its entirety
And then it is gone
And onto the next moment
And it starts all over again
Moment by moment
Gently unfolding
Always there to experience
For you to choose
How to accept
The special moment
It is yours for the asking
Anything is possible
Belief and trust are the foundation
The building blocks
To new horizons
To fuller moments
To enhancing everything around you
Belief in yourself
Belief in the way things are
Belief that everything is the way it should be
Trusting, believing and accepting
Accepting the past
Embracing the present
Believing in the future
It is all possible
The peace and harmony
Are all around
It starts within
Then slowly spreads
Like a spider
Spinning its web

Piece by piece

Until it is bigger

And bigger

So it is with you

The web will increase in size

To keep you safe

And supported

And loved

It's all a web

And we are all connected

Strand by strand

One piece at a time

You cannot see the strands

But they are there

Joining us

Like hands join lovers

Or mothers and children

The web is perfect

It unites us

And radiates out

And out and out

Further than you can imagine

Joining one and all

On all planes

At all levels

It is an intricate web

Never to be broken

Growing stronger

As your trust grows

And you experience it

Each strand taking you in a different direction

But each strand linked to the web
To bring it all together
In perfect harmony
The spider diligently spins its web
Starting with nothing
But knowing instinctively that it will be a web
So, too must you instinctively believe
The web is there
It is up to you to make the connections
One strand at a time
Believing it is possible
Accepting it
And embracing it
One by one
The connections are there
It is up to you
To receive them
So close
Yet so far
Open up to the possibilities
You will feel things
You have never felt
You will experience
The ecstasy
Of knowing
It all fits together
Perfectly
No illusions
No mistakes
It is the way it is
Reach out

It is there for you
Moment by moment
Inch by inch
The web will grow
With you at the center
Of your web
And all else surrounding you
So much to explore
So much to learn
All in due course
No rush to be
Just being
Is all there is
And acceptance
Of that being
And all the possibilities

Belief in yourself
Belief in the way things are
Belief that everything is the
way it should be
Trusting, believing and accepting
Accepting the past
Embracing the present
Believing in the future

THE SUN RISES

The dawn is the sign of a new day

So fresh

The dew on the ground

Signaling the overnight mist

And the new day breaks

The sun is rising

As it always does

To sweep over you for another day

And then to set again

Perfect timing every day

Day in and day out

The sun rises

And then it sets

Showing her brightness

In different parts

At different times

But always constant

As the sun sets

So do you know

That it will rise

In all her splendor

The next day

The predictability of the rising sun

Is like all patterns in life

We rise up

And we fall down

Only to rise again

Life goes on

And so must you
At times wanting to just rest
But needing to rise
Fulfilling the promise of the day ahead
Day in
Day out
Tasks to be done
Tasks to be learned
It is all part of the circle
Of the journey
No beginning
And no end
Just perfect and right
Wherever you are
In the circle
Contributing to all circles
Which are in their own perfection

We rise up
And we fall down
Only to rise again

THE CALENDAR

The pages of the calendar
Show the passing of another year
So relevant to you on your plane
A new chapter
A new beginning
A time of renewal
A time to move ahead
Remember the past
It has cherished memories
And so much wonder
But embrace today
For it is the center
It is the beginning
Of new tomorrows
Of new memories
Today is the start line
Be ready for the signals
To move on
To awaken to all around you
The path has a start
It is the beginning
Today is where it all begins
Do not worry about the finish line
Make it to the start
And let it flow
Look forward
Not back
There is so much out there
For you to embrace

PARADISE

The most beautiful painting
In your imagination
Cannot begin to describe
The beauty of this dimension
It is paradise
Whatever the heart desires
The eyes can behold
It is a multi-colored garden
It is a crystal clear lake
A beautiful sunset
A starry night
A green meadow
A beautiful mountain
It is a panorama of the heart's desire
Not only to look at
But, the sounds
They are a symphony
Of harmonies
Blending into the landscape
The music part of the whole
Completing the picture
The colors – magnificent
In their richness and hues
It is perfection
The plants in full bloom
The colors intermingling
Creating a celebration
Of their being
It is paradise

NOW IS ALL THERE IS

A new dawn has broken
The rapture of new beginnings
The key to a new dawning
The hope lies eternal
In each new sunrise
A new beginning
A gentle unfolding
Of daylight
The promise of new things
Of hopes and dreams
The new day holds that
And more
A time to give
And a time to receive
A time to be busy
And a time to be still
A time to work
And a time to play
This the day holds
And more
It all starts at the beginning
And builds on that
One block at a time
No rush to get there
All in due course
Now is everything
Now is the essence
Now is the focus

Focus on the now
For that is the key
Life is a series of nows
Each now building on the next
It is how you live in the now
That determines your yesterdays
And your tomorrows
So even though you relate
That you only have a
Short block of time
It is here for you
To see
What you can do in a short time
A simple message
A short poem
The message is clear
Now is all there is

Now is everything
Now is the essence
Now is the focus
Focus on the now
For that is the key

THE ROAD

The road to wellness
Is not a straight line
The twists and curves
Are random and scattered
Sometimes uphill
Other times downhill
At times a level course
But always the road forges ahead
Sometimes it appears to be a dead-end
But there is always a way
The means is the way
The path is there to choose
So simple, so easy
It beckons
A giant hurdle to overcome
But worth the effort
One step at a time
The power to resist
To fight
To succumb
The choice is there
For you to make
To let it flow
All in due course
The obstacles seem insurmountable
The course so hard
The finish line so hazy
But, it starts with the first step

One small step
Is all it takes
One step at a time
Slowly, methodically
Moving forward
Is all there is
Is all there can be

But, it starts with the first step
One small step
Is all it takes
One step at a time

YOU ARE THE FORCE

The light surrounds you
And captures you
In all its shining glory
You are the essence
Of love, light and wisdom
The light from within
And the light from around
Merging as one
Captivating and holding
The love all around
Beckoning you forward
Surrounding and leading you
To greater visions
And understanding
So much known already
So much to know
Trusting, believing
Integrating it all
You are the center
You are the light
You are the beginning
And the end
You are all things
And more
You are the force
The driving force
To making it happen
It is in your grasp

If you allow it to flow
No resistance
Just accepting the flow
Of life's events
One step at a time
I am with you
On your journey
Guiding, leading
Waiting to teach
To share
To help you experience
What you need to know
Always waiting
Always willing
Always ready
Yours for the asking
It is all here for you
So simple
So splendid
So glorious
Together we can be
In all time
The bond so strong
And strengthening
Through understanding
The bridge is coming together
Bridging the two of us
Back and forth
You can go
Knowing the bridge
Will forever unite us

THE FLICKER OF LIGHT

The questions are raised
The doubts persist
The unknown world
So uncomfortable
And threatening
To the unenlightened
Their time will arrive
When they too are willing
And receptive
To seeing the light
To choosing the way
The barriers will diminish
The questions will be answered
When the time is right
A time in the dark
And a time in the light
Once the light is there
Even if only a flicker
No retreating into the darkness
The flicker of light
Will continue to grow
In strength and size
In brightness
Surrounding and encompassing
All around you
A gift to bask in
To spread
And to share

Soaking up the light
The rays
The knowledge
The awareness
It is the key
To unlocking the vaults
Of the unknown

*The questions will be answered
When the time is right*

THE BOND

The memories
The foundations of yesteryear
The joy in remembering
In sharing
In reminiscing
In feeling
And in feeling we are always united
Together in thought
In spirit
In love and in light
Always here
Not just a memory
But a forever bond
So close
So together
So united
We are all one
Separated by a thin thread
A thought
Brings us together in total harmony
The vibrations
The energy
The wave lengths
Enabling the process
Facilitating the flow
Of words, thoughts and teachings
You are the receptor
Of our teachings

There is so much to receive
So much to give
To share
To accept and understand
Taking the time
Is the beginning
Of the flow of information
To better understanding
Knowledge and wisdom
Always here for you
You have the key
To open the gateway
To understanding
Always here for you
Always waiting patiently
For your signal
For your readiness
For your love
Together it is possible
For you to enter
The gateway
You feel the light
All around you
You bask in the light
You are the light

ALWAYS HERE FOR YOU

I am at your side
Together we stride
I feel your breath
I know your energy
Always here for you
Waiting for you
To share all I have to teach
To open your eyes
Your heart
Your spirit
There is no beginning
And there is no end
Just a continuum
An ever flowing circle
Of love and light
We are all part of the circle
At different degrees
In different levels
But we are all connected
Our lives intertwined
Attached together
At all times
We are so close
In some senses
Yet the sense of closeness
As you on your plane
Know closeness
Is not there

It is a deeper closeness
We are always together
Connected through all time
At all levels
In all dimensions
You feel the energy
And know
It is real

There is no beginning
And there is no end
Just a continuum
An ever flowing circle
Of love and light

ALL ACCORDING TO PLAN

It is always a timely passing
It is as it should be
Not a moment too soon
Not a second too late
It is all according to plan
No mistakes
No accidents
It is as it should be
Every person passing at the right time
For that person
It does not end at passing
But is another step of the journey
Each passing a new beginning
In another dimension
It is all according to plan

It is all according to plan
No mistakes
No accidents
It is as it should be

THE FLAME

The candle flickers
And seems to dance
This way and that
Higher and lower
Constantly changing
I am the flame
I am the light
I am the source
I am vibrant
I am energy
I am
Here with you
In this moment
And beyond
United
Always together
Through all eternity
Through this season
And the next
Through this year
And the next
And the following
United in time
United in place
In all places
Through eternity
Time is meaningless
It is but an instant

In the scope of all there is
It is a never-ending journey
Of learning and discovery
And understanding.
The key is love
It is the gateway
To hope
To joy
To enhanced living
Love is the answer
Love for everything
And everyone
It is the thread
That unites
And joins
It all together.

The key is love
It is the gateway
To hope
To joy
To enhanced living
Love is the answer

THE COMPASS

The love and energy
Surround you
The light dances
And circles around you
You are in the light
You are the light
Let the light radiate in
Let the light radiate out
Feel the light
Capture it and hold it
And share the light
Making it brighter
Live in the light
Out of the darkness
The light beckons
The light calls
The light sustains
And fills you
To overflowing
The glow is eternal
It is all encompassing
Bask in the light
And feel the love
All around you
The compass shows which direction to go
North, south, east or west
A simple tool
Fulfilling a huge need
The compass points the way
Assisting when you are lost

It shows the way
It is so easy
Sometimes in life
The direction in which you are heading
Seems uncertain
You don't have a compass
To point you the right way
Look inside yourself
For guidance, for help
Intuition – what a beautiful word
It is in you
To find the way
At times you may veer off course
But your intuition brings you back
It centers you
It steers you
In the direction you need to go
You need to trust
To surrender
To ask for guidance
Go within for the answers
They're within you
You have the answers
All you need do is ask
You are your own compass
If you have faith
And believe in yourself
Trust what you feel
And have the courage
To go in the direction
Your compass is pointing
Each person has their own unique compass

Follow your own dreams
Do what is right for you
Believe it is possible
Listen to your inner voice
The answers are there
Let your compass
Show you the way
It is the right way for you
For you, it is the only way
On your journey

You need to trust
To surrender
To ask for guidance
Go within for the answers
They're within you
You have the answers
All you need do is ask

YOU ARE THE ESSENCE

Time
There is no beginning
And there is no end
It is a circle
There is no start line
There is no finish
Time is the undercurrent
That keeps moving
It is constant
It is always moving
On your plane it is said
Time is of the essence
But it should really be
You are of the essence
Without you at the center,
Time as you know it
Is meaningless
You are what is important
Finding the time
Is really about
Finding you
At times, it feels
Like time is at a standstill
Treasure those moments
When you are so in the moment
Time seems to fall away
And all there is, is now
That moment of being in that moment
Is the key to being
Of being ever-present

EBB AND FLOW

The ebb and flow of life
Sometimes slow
Sometimes fast
Move with the flow
Recognize there will be times
That not all goals
Are accomplished
At times it seems effortless
That you are in the flow
And it appears so easy
At other times
There will be obstacles
Treat the obstacles
As your friends
They too have a message for you
Learn from the hardships
They enrich your experience
Teach you compassion
And enable you to see
The other side
Strive for the balance
Appreciating the good
And what you feel
Is not so good
For in every experience
There are lessons to be learnt
Greater understanding will evolve
Over the course of time

Of the ebb and flow
We all experience
At nightfall there is darkness
And just as surely as there is darkness
The daybreak of a new dawn
Will herald in light
And the hope of a new day
So it is with life
At times it will appear
As if there is only darkness
But out of the darkness
Comes light
And some new gifts
Gifts of appreciation
Gifts of wisdom
Gifts of compassion
And the gift of understanding
The light is here
For all who seek
The plentiful gifts
So abundant
Waiting to enrich
Your life
Balancing the light and the dark
One of the keys to love
Right here for you

The daybreak of a new dawn
Will herald in light
And the hope of a new day
So it is with life
At times it will appear
As if there is only darkness
But out of the darkness
Comes light

THE TAPESTRY

The tapestry of life
Is woven of many fine threads
The stitches so carefully crafted
Each stitch worthy of the next
Each stitch able to stand alone
But, so much more beautiful
As part of the whole
Together the stitches
Create a masterpiece
Beautiful for the eyes to behold
Enriching the senses
In every way
So, it is with life
It is the small, mundane events
That give life its beauty
And the meaning of life
Is found in the ordinary things
The key is the ability
To find the beauty
And the richness
In the day to day
You can unlock the door
And live in the beauty
And splendor that is before you

THE PEACH AND THE WATERFALL

The juice of the peach

Runneth over

So sweet

First you need to bite

To savor the taste

To smell the aroma

To feel the texture

Without the first bite

It is difficult to experience

The juice of the peach

So it is with life

You need to live it

To experience it

To feel it

By standing on the sidelines

And watching

Is not the same as doing

As being

Be a part of life

Be in your life

Feel it, experience it

But don't let it pass you by

Be open to the joy

Of every experience

Let the experiences

Cascade over you

Like a free-falling waterfall

Be in the flow of the water

Be part of the beauty
Flowing freely
Over time and distance
And space
Doing only what a waterfall does
Naturally
In all her splendor
Be a part of life
Be a part of your life
Take a stance
Make it happen
You are the center
You are in the controls
You need to steer the way
You have the power
To go in any direction
The choice is all yours
All yours for the asking
All you need do is ask

Be open to the joy
Of every experience
Let the experiences
Cascade over you
Like a free-falling waterfall

EACH DAY IS A GIFT

The essence of life is change
And having the ability
To flow through the changes
Life is never constant
But it is in a constant change of flux
Changes spurt growth
Changes encourage learning
Changes command thinking
And it is through thought
That you are transformed
To higher levels of learning
The path of life
Is never a smooth one
There will be detours on the road
Some detours will appear good
And beyond your most wonderful dreams
Other detours will appear bad
But, all detours are stepping-stones
On the road of life
To learning the lessons
That were inscribed for you
Each day is a gift
To embrace and welcome
Some days there will be good gifts
That bring joy, happiness and peace
Other days will bring "bad" gifts
That bring hardship, pain and suffering
But within each gift

There are lessons to be learned
And it is through these lessons
Which are at times difficult to bear
That the greatest transformation will take place
Think back on your life
And how the hard times
Propelled you to higher levels
And brought you to new ground
To a new way of thinking
To an altered state of perception
To live life fully
Entails encompassing the good and the bad
Experiencing the full spectrum of emotions
If life had only good experiences
There would be too much living in the comfort zone
Too much complacency and expectation
The apparent negative experiences
Enable life to have meaning
And this balancing of good and bad
Enhances your appreciation
And understanding of life

Each day is a gift
To embrace and welcome

THE PLANTING OF THE SEEDS

The journey of life

Is never a straight path

There will inevitably be detours

And stops along the way

The power is within you

To make the changes

To discover

New horizons

Along a different path

The key is to have the courage

To confront the unknown

Facing the uncertainty

With strength and faith

There is a better way

The hurdles will be there for you to conquer

There will be missteps along the way

The path will not always be smooth

There will be tremendous learning

And there will be growth

You will flower

Just like the seed takes time to flourish

So too will your dreams take time

Nurture your dreams

Inspire your passion

Give it your commitment

Out of your dedication

The flowers will blossom

And spread abundantly

Reaching areas you can hardly imagine
The planting of the seeds
Is the first step to cultivating the dream
It is a process
Requiring your spirit
Which will soar
As the seeds begin to flourish
Let go of expectations
Live in the flow of the moment
Be conscious of all around you
There is a wealth of goodness
And love around you
Open up to the love
Let the light shine in
This is the beginning of a new venture
But it is the path for which you
Were destined to travel
There are no mysteries
It is finding the way
To your life's work
Everything is intertwined
Everything has a purpose
All the events of the past
Relevant to who you are today
Without all your yesteryears
You would not be the person you have become
Or the person you will be
The road reaches out to meet you
It is waiting for you
To embark on the journey
To take you to a new tomorrow

Filled with passion, love and joy
New doors will open for you
As you close other doors behind you
Do not look back
As the future is bright and clear
Your focus is the key
To unlocking the doors
That stand before you
You carry the key
And only you can unlock
The promise of the future
I am here to write with you
Pages, chapters, books
They are all possible
With your dedication
The connection will flourish
And the teachings will flow
To your pen, to the written word
You will share the writings
In your quest for the truth

Let go of expectations
Live in the flow of the moment

THE GIFTS OF THE UNIVERSE

Open yourself up to all there is out there. The universe has so much abundance to share with you. The lessons unfolding one by one, all in their own time. Never too soon, never too late, and always in perfect sequence. There are no mistakes. At times it may appear that life is harsh but there is always a purpose behind the suffering. Out of the suffering comes awakening and understanding. A deeper perception and appreciation of the life you lead. Joy evolves out of your experience with sadness and makes the joyful experience that much more meaningful. It is against the backdrop of difficult times and living through the pain that growth occurs. The light is always there to sustain and guide you. Open your heart to the gifts of the Universe for they are plentiful and waiting to be savored. The passageway to awareness is a gradual awakening of the senses. Each sense combining and working in harmony to produce full awareness and understanding of life. The steps at times appear too steep to ascend – it is at that exact time and moment when you need to trust the most and to surrender yourself. It is through this process of letting go that you will find yourself and the courage to ascend higher. The more you fight it, the harder the struggle and the deeper the suffering. Surrender to the possibilities and the rewards will be there for you to experience. The thought of change evokes feelings of fear, anticipation and the unknown. You need to embrace the fear and surrender to it. Let the fear guide you and lead you. Fear is a wonderful teacher if you choose to embrace and confront it. By not confronting the fear you will be stuck in one place. It takes strength and courage to confront the fear and face it head on – but it is the only way to get through the fear and to develop the insight. So many lessons to be learned along the way. Take advantage of the opportunities placed in your way, whether they are positive or negative, they will aid your growth

The universe has so much abundance to share with you. The lessons unfolding one by one, all in their own time. Never too soon, never too late, and always in perfect sequence

THE HOURGLASS

The day is yet young
Time is not running out
The sands of time in the hourglass
Slowly trickle through
Each particle of sand
Contributing to time elapsing
Serving as a symbol of time
Many particles representing a second
Making the most of precious moments
A second is a moment in time
Yet each second so significant
It only takes a second
To make a choice
Yet the choice made in that second
Can have ramifications for a lifetime
Your life is but an instant
Spanning across many dimensions

It only takes a second
To make a choice
Yet the choice made in that second
Can have ramifications for a lifetime

CHANGE

Change can happen gradually
Like the ocean ebbing and flowing
Against the sand dunes
Transforming over time
The gentle currents slowly invoke changes
On the ocean floor
Almost impossible to see the changes
But they have occurred
Gently, passively and in perfect harmony
Day after day
Month after month
Year after year
Sculpting the ocean bed
And creating miniscule changes
That are difficult to discern
Below the depths of the ocean
The changes in nature
Do not happen haphazardly
They are tuned into the cycles of the moon
Following the command of Mother Earth
And doing things they are meant to do
No questioning
No hesitation
Just doing.
But change can also happen suddenly
Without warning
Changes can erupt and transform everything in an instant
That nothing appears the same as it was before

Earthquakes, hurricanes, typhoons and tornadoes
Can wreak havoc on those who were affected
They happen so suddenly
Slamming into people's lives
And changing the landscape of how things used to be
Yet they are part of nature
Part of those gentle currents
And soft breezes
Yet sometimes they bring danger and death
And change is inevitable

The changes in nature
Do not happen haphazardly
They are tuned into the cycles of the moon
Following the command of Mother Earth
And doing things they are meant to do
No questioning
No hesitation
Just doing

ROAD OF LIFE

Experiences in life change people
As in nature, the changes can be gradual or sudden
Some people appear unchanged by the changes
Whilst others are transformed by the changes
Each person reacting in their own way
Such a personal journey
And every person traversing their life
In their own personal way
The road of life has predestined plans
And along the journey
Each person will face forks in the road
And decisions will be made
That will affect the rest of the journey
And determine the way for that person
There will be right turns and what appear
To be wrong detours
But there will be no mistakes
As each turn will offer the chance for growth
A detour may not appear to be the right
Way to where you are going
But eventually you will arrive
And be changed by the detour
There are so many questions to be asked
And there are so many answers
There is much to be shared
The time is now
To move forward
On your continuing journey
Along the road of life

LIVE THIS DAY

The tides of time
Ebb and flow
The unfolding weeks
Turn into months
And on your plane
The page of the calendar turns
To a new month
Each day with a corresponding date
So relevant in your dimension
Dates symbolizing significant milestones
Dates symbolizing diverse memories
Dates have meaning and purpose
You look forward and with anticipation
To certain days in the calendar
Yet each day is symbolic
This day is all there is
Living in this moment
Living life to the fullest
This day is the beginning
Live this day
As if it were your first
Live this day
As if it were your last
Live it with purpose
Live it in spirit
Live it with spirit
This day is here
And then it is gone
Be in this day
All that you can be

THE TUNNEL

At times on the journey
It will feel as if you are going through a tunnel
You are unable to see the other side
You know it is there when you are in the tunnel
But can't see it
Everything in the tunnel is dark
You know there was an entrance
You know there is an exit
Yet in the middle
You appear to be neither here nor there
You are in between
You know if you keep going
The tunnel will end
And you will enter daylight
So it is with this journey
That you have embarked on
You have entered the tunnel
You are traveling to the other side
You can't go back to the entrance
You are in-between
Reaching for the exit of the tunnel
For greater understanding
But first having to travel the tunnel
The journey is wrought with questions
And anticipation of the answers
The tunnel is a series of teachings
Enabling you to get to the other side
Where light and love are so bright

Where lightness and darkness co-exist
There are many tunnels
Along the path
Each tunnel leading to a deeper connection
And a better perception
And understanding
Along the Road of Life

The tunnel is a series of teachings
Enabling you to get to the other side
Where light and love are so bright
Where lightness and darkness co-exist

CAPTURE THE MOMENT

The picture captures the joy
It is captivating
The joy shines through
A picture says a thousand words
It goes straight to the essence
The lens of the camera
Captures the heart of the moment
And then the photo
Is always a moment in time
Remembering the moments
By gazing at photos
Reminiscing about days gone by
The good old days
Yet how often were you not present
In that snapshot in time
That is now a memory of a lifetime
The photos are a partial time line
Of the life you have lived
The life you live
And the life that you will live
Clicking away on special days
And on ordinary ones, too
Trying to capture the moment
That has come and gone
The photo being a keepsake of treasured memories
Of special dreams
Of life going by
Day by day

The photos remind you
Of all that has gone by
Yet serve to show
How far you have come
Each year documented
And recorded
For posterity
Yet, what is posterity
It is the future
It is the past
It is the present
It is an intermingling of the three
You are the posterity
Of those who came before you
And the cycle continues
Through your life
In your life
And after your life
A chain never to be broken
The continuum of life
Goes on and on
Through generations before
And those that will follow
So too does your life go on
In other dimensions
In other realms
Yet it continues
On into posterity
And way beyond
There are no "true" pictures
To capture life in this dimension

There are artists' renderings
And soaring imaginations
But this truth would be impossible
To capture through the lens of a camera
It is multi-dimensional
It is multi-faceted
It is indescribable beauty
It has such depth
And such clarity
It is a wonder to behold
The colors blend in perfect harmony
To depict a masterpiece
This is perfection in the true sense
Absolutely nothing is amiss
It is a feast for the eyes and all the senses
It truly is paradise

Yet, what is posterity
It is the future
It is the past
It is the present
It is an intermingling of the three

ASK FOR WHAT YOU WANT

The pages of the calendar
Turn and herald a new beginning
A new dawn has broken
And with it a sense of renewal
A new year beckons
And opportunities abound
There for you to seize
Take advantage of the gifts
That are yours for the taking
You have the chance
If only you ask
It all begins with asking
Ask for what you want
First you need to determine
Your inner yearnings
And then ask, ask, ask
The paths will open
Welcoming you into their embrace
As you live the life you have chosen
Pursue it with passion
Embracing it
And acknowledging it was all
That you asked it to be
There is a new beginning
A time for rejuvenation
A time for reenergizing
A time to be
All you want to be

THE JOY IS IN THE LIVING

The stillness of the night

Heralds a new dawning

Daybreak – a time of new beginnings

A fresh start

Sunrise – a time of hope

The start of a new day

A time for living

A time for loving

A time of joy

Each day offers this and more

Beckoning you to grasp it

To enjoy the day

Savor it

For each day to be lived

It must be experienced

The joy is in the living

So many minutes tucked into the day

Yet the day has finite minutes

Before night falls

Make those minutes count

They are precious

They are here

And all too soon they are gone

The days slip into oblivion

But if you choose to live in the minute

This minute, like the last minute

Will not be in vain

This minute will count

It will be remembered

As all your precious minutes should be remembered

Each day is the opportunity

To make the most of time as you know it

Slow down

Savor this instant

For it is here

But now it is already gone

And so the next instant

Will be gone

And so it goes

That each instant

Passes into the past

Transforming those seconds into something meaningful

Gives life purpose

Accounting for the time

Brings balance to life

Know that no life is in vain

Each has a purpose

A mission

Unique to the soul of that person

Every soul fulfills their mission

All in their own time

Know that no life is in vain
Each has a purpose
A mission
Unique to the soul of that person

ABANDON YOUR GUILT

Guilt is not an emotion

That will take you to the next level

So abandon your guilt

And embrace the light

The light will lead you

To higher levels

In a purposeful and forthright way

Guilt is self-defeating

And serves no purpose

Abandon any guilt feelings

And move forward

Your energy will be transformed

Into positive thoughts

These will invoke actions

To propel you forward

Not holding you back

The time is now

To act

Not to react

To move

Not to stagnate

To live

Not to die

To love

Not to hate

Now is the time

For you

TOGETHER AS ONE

Singing with such joy
The notes crescend
At different levels
Different pitches
The voices harmonize
All singing different tunes
But together the melody
Becomes one
All the voices
United in song
The notes coming together
In unity
Together as one
So it is with you and me
We are together
We sing different notes
Hear different tunes
But we sing together
To make a perfect tune
Without you
The tune cannot sound
It needs your voice
To complete the melody
We wait for you
With our arms open wide
To sing all the songs
Waiting to be sung
Together

CELEBRATE THE MOMENT

Let time pass as it may
Let the new dawn break
A new beginning
A new horizon
It is a new day
Let regrets not taint today
For they do not belong
No purpose to be served
By regretting what could have been
Concern yourself with what is
And be only in this moment
Live this moment fully
Absorbing all that it encompasses
Smell the sweetness
Savor this moment
Because all too quickly
This too shall pass
You are promised nothing
Only this moment
So celebrate the moment
And let it be
All that it can be
Seize it in its entirety
Appreciate the opportunity
To capture the essence
That this moment alone
Can hold for you
However, the moment can be lost

But hold no regrets
For that lost moment
For instantly there is a new moment
To seize
To experience
To expand in that moment
In essence that is the essence of life
Seizing the moment
And living in this instant moment
Not dwelling on the past
Not dreaming about the future
But being fully in the present
This is all there is
It is such an easy concept
Yet so hard to grasp
Children are masters of life
They are life teachers
Able to be so present
In the here and now
Children live in the moment
It is so simple
Yet it is so complex
Now is all you have
So let it be meaningful
Let it enrich you
Let it encircle you
Let now be all you ever need
For this is life
A series of nows
You move from now to then
But concern yourself only with now

Give it your full attention
Whatever you choose to do
Do it with your full heart
Your full attention
Just live in the now
It is so very simple

Now is all you have
So let it be meaningful
Let it enrich you
Let it encircle you
Let now be all you ever need

LEAP OF FAITH

Life sometimes appears unpredictable
But what does that mean?
That events didn't transpire
According to how you envisioned
Yet everything happens
According to plan
Sometimes it is hard to imagine
Why things turn out the way they do
We try to understand
We question
We analyze
Yet we cannot find the answers
It is a huge leap of faith
To realize that the exact way
Things do turn out
Is exactly according to plan
You may ask "How can that be?"
To which the simple answer
Would be
It is all according to plan

IT IS IN YOUR POWER

Life is a cycle
There is no beginning
There is no end
It is a continuum
That is ever lasting
It is so simple
Yet it is so complex
Understanding and believing
Are keys to the safe
The safe holds the knowledge
To understanding and believing
So it is a cycle
One perpetuating the other
It is a leap of faith
To believe
To know
To understand
The essence to knowing
Is always there for you
It is in your power
To tap into that which is in you
It is yours for the taking
It is yours for the asking
You hold the power
You hold the key
To all you need to know

TRUST YOUR INNER WISDOM

The mind minds the message
An open mind is magnificent
Allowing new thoughts to enter
And proceed into your reality
But what is real?
What is reality?
Your reality is that which resonates
As true to you
It is a feeling of comfort
Of safety of being home
Your truth is that which feels
Right to you
You need to trust your truth
It is your soul speaking directly to you
Trust your inner wisdom
You know your own truth
You cannot live by the truth of another
As that is their truth
Only your truth will resonate to your core
For it is your personal truth
So often we walk a path
That is a combination of different truths
However, at your core
You know the truth that is best for you
Listen to yourself
Be still
Quiet your mind
Be receptive
Slow down
Be open

It is all there for you
Waiting to be grasped
Waiting to be absorbed
Waiting to be accepted
Waiting to be practiced
You know the truth
It is within you
It is without you
It is all around you
Embrace it
Feel it
Conquer it
Your truth will free you
To do all you need to do
Your truth will inspire you
To reach your highest good
To reach that for which you were created
To be the true you
You are unlike any other being
And no being is like you
That is what makes you special
Aspire to be only you
Because that is all you were meant to be
Only you
Nobody else
It all begins with trust

You need to trust your truth
It is your soul speaking directly to you

LISTEN TO YOUR INNER VOICE

This is a new beginning for you

Do not look back

Only look ahead

At all that awaits you

Look at this moment

Feel what you are feeling

Experience this present moment

For you have made a choice

A decision that will steer you

In a new direction

Opportunities will open up to you

Keep your heart open

Trust your instincts

Listen to your inner voice

You have the power

To access your inner wisdom

Listen

Stop

Breathe

Be still

Be quiet

Let your wisdom guide you

On your own personal journey

By listening to your heart

Your soul will be alight

And let you be

All that you are intended to be

The future awaits

With open arms
But it is how you deal with
This present moment
That determines what the future
Has in store for you
Your actions today
Will determine your tomorrows
So be present in this moment
To reap the kind of tomorrow
You dream about
It has been said since the
Beginning of time
Ask and you shall receive
And so it is
Know what you want
Ask for it
Dream it
Be it
And live it
It is all there for the asking

Let your wisdom guide you
On your own personal journey
By listening to your heart
Your soul will be alight
And let you be
All that you are intended to be

LINKED IN ALL ETERNITY

Life is a cycle
Of welcomes and farewells
Tasting the familiar
Returning to one's roots
The past embraces the future
The future embraces the past
They are both intertwined
Linked in all eternity
The familiar and the unfamiliar
Coming together in unity
So complex yet so very simple
The mysteries of the universe
The end is the beginning
The beginning is the end
And so it is a cycle
Of continuous replenishment
It ends at the start
And begins at the finish
Yet it is forever a circle
Of continuum
A circle that grows forever
A circle that enlarges
And expands
A circle that embraces
A circle that enfolds
Stepping into the circle
Stepping out of the circle
Life is a series of steps

Sometimes the steps

Seem out of sequence

Yet they are always

Surmounted in the order

They need to be climbed

At times to you

It appears as though

In your world

You ascend a few steps

Only to descend a couple of steps

Yet you are always reaching

Ascending and growing

It is not a straight line

But an upward circle

That you are able to transcend

In time in space in life

In eternity

I am the circle

You are the circle

We are the circle

Together we are embraced

Together we are encapsulated

Different levels of the circle

Different parts of the circle

So evident to us

We are in the circle

We are all safe

And so it goes

Round and round

Up and up

Up and round

Round and up
Circles and circles
Upwards and onwards
In all eternity

The past embraces the future
The future embraces the past
They are both intertwined
Linked in all eternity

THE ROSE

Each of us has our own journey
To travel
Each of us our path to travel
There are thorns to be encountered
And roses to be smelled
At times it seems as though
The rose bush is one of only thorns
And life seems harsh and unfair
It is difficult to see the rose
When all one feels are the thorns
Yet the rose is always
Waiting to bloom
The rose is growing and waiting
For the right time
For the right place
For the right conditions
To start the process
Of budding
Of growing
Of becoming all it is meant to be
A beautiful rose
Sometimes the conditions for the rose
Do not enable it to bud
So it is not seen
But the rose is always waiting
To bloom
Now the conditions are right
The thorns have protected the

Blooming of the rose for all
This time
The rose now blooms
The rose now grows
The rose is precious

Each of us has our own journey
To travel
Each of us our path to travel

THE TREE

The leaves of the trees
Are in full bloom
Despite the heat of the summer
They continue to grow and flourish
Succulent greens of all colors
The leaves stay steadfastly to the branches
Growing and developing
A leaf on its own
In the singular
Is not so spectacular
But the accumulation of all the leaves
Together on the branches
Is a thing of beauty
To behold
The leaves are all branches
Of the tree
That grows
That blows
That knows
How to grow
How to bud
How to develop
The leaves know when it is time
To fall
To drop off the branches
So that the tree
Can retreat for the winter
Only to bud and blossom

In the springtime
Again and again
And so the leaves of the tree
Return
Time after time
Year in
Year out
The tree grows all the time
Despite the fact
It appears at times as if
The tree is not living
So it is with
The family tree
There is growth and development
And then there is a time
Of cutting back
Of falling off the tree
So it appears as if
Branches of the family tree
Cease to be
But it is not so
The tree is always there
Branching in different directions
Growing and scaling back
At different times
But always growing
As life intends it to grow
Different leaves grow
They are part of the same tree
Yet each leaf is
Unique in its entirety

Sharing the same branch
Each leaf is different
Then the other leaves on the branch
So it is too with families
Time after time
The roots are the same
But the uniqueness of
Each individual
Makes each one special
And even though similarities
Are apparent
It is the singularity
That is so special
Just as the individual
Leaf on the tree
Is not so spectacular
So too is the individual
Seen in isolation
Not so special
It is the relationships
Of the individual
Among other individuals
That allows the individual
To grow
To flourish
To become all it needs to be
It is in the family tree
That the individual
Becomes all that it was intended to be
Not in isolation
But as a branch

Of the tree
All the branches
Work in harmony
Coming together
Working together
The branches of the tree
Blow and grow together
So it is with you
Always part of a tree
Your past is the future
Your future is the past
So it is for
All eternity

It is the relationships
Of the individual
Among other individuals
That allows the individual
To grow
To flourish
To become all it needs to be

HAVEN OF HEALING

There is a sense of calm
There is a knowledge of belonging
There is peace
There is joy
There is serenity
The haven of healing
Is so sacred
Peace infiltrates
Surrounding and fulfilling
There is warmth
Where there was cold
There is peace
Where there was agitation
There is love
Where there was emptiness
There is joy
Where there was sadness
The circle of love
Continues
The circle of love
Enfolds
There is harmony
There is healing
There is hope
For this is home
And all is safe

ELEMENTS OF NATURE

The rain falls relentlessly
The harsh winds blow
The elements of nature
Are not to be reckoned
The pouring rain
Beats down faster and faster
There is no letting up
The rain keeps falling
Torrential
There is no way to stop the rain
For this is nature
At its finest
We cannot control nature
But need to live
Side by side
And within nature
Fire and water
Two strong elements
Both so necessary
Yet both can be so dangerous
When taken to the extreme
The fires wrecked havoc
On many lands
Yet hurricanes too have
Caused havoc
To many
Fire and water
Necessary elements

With which we cannot live without
Yet taken to the extreme
They cause loss of lives
And upheaval

We cannot control nature
But need to live
Side by side
And within nature

SILVER LINING

There is always a silver lining
In every situation
A reason that too often
Is not apparent to
The human eye
Even in the darkest clouds
There are specks of joy
Out of the darkness
Comes light
Just as day
Always follows night
At time it feels as though
Life is devoid of joy
And happy times
Are not a possibility
It feels like the bottom
Has been reached
And there is nothing to
Laugh about
Yet it is in these gloomy moments
That one comes to know one's self
To test your strength
Your courage
Your true self
And how through the depths of despair
The goodness and kindness
Of the human spirit truly shines
For it is by encountering hardship

That one is truly able
To appreciate the good times
Nobody is immune from tragedy
Bringing grace and dignity
To the trying moments
Helps one to rise above
And feel stronger
To face the next hurdle
One is sure to encounter
On the journey of life
There will be days of laughter
And there will be days of tears
Both serve a dual function
And in their duality are joined
The emotions of laughter and crying
Are linked
Both serve as a release
Of pent-up feelings
Of letting go
Of release
And any time you release
Your feelings
You are open
To the human experience
Of living and loving
Of opening your heart
Of sharing
Both joy and sadness
Sometimes when things appear
Especially bleak
It seems hard to envision

There will ever be a reason to laugh
But one has to trust
That everything has a purpose
And that out of the deepest sorrow
Often emerges the most profound joy
Without experiencing the sorrow
The joy would not be the same
Imagine a life devoid of
Pain and suffering
Of joy and laughter
Of just living a mediocre life
Without these feelings
Each one has their place
In the life cycle
Each will be encountered
At different stages
To different degrees
In your lifetime
Each interlude with grief
Has a silver lining
As when the grief lifts
There is so much to behold
However, sans the grief
There would be no joy
Just moving along
In a robotic manner
Laughter is the key to the soul
As sadness is key to the heart
They are united
And the key switches back and forth
Opening the heart and the soul

To all the beauty
To all the ecstasy
Of living in the world
Difficult as it is to believe
One needs to trust
One needs to know
That the dark days will
Be followed by sunshine
For light always prevails

Even in the darkest clouds
There are specks of joy
Out of the darkness
Comes light
Just as day
Always follows night

LESSONS

Each lesson has a message
Or many messages to be shared
Some messages will resonate
With some people
Immediately
While other messages
May take time
And reflection
Before they can be understood
And ingested
Just as certain foods
Need to be savored
To appreciate
All the tastes
Within the food
So, too, will certain lessons
Need to slowly be savored
Some foods
Are an acquired taste
And may not be
Appreciated immediately
So, too, will it be with some messages
They may need to be read
And reread
Before they are understood
Many messages will be
So simple
And easy to grasp
For some people

Yet other people
Will have a harder time
Grasping these messages
Yet understanding other messages
With no problems
So these teachings
Will benefit each person
In a different way
There is no right way
There is no wrong way
There is only the way
That is right
For each individual
Some people will laugh at the lessons
Some people will cry
Again each person
Will react in their own unique way
To the writings
And the lessons
These are meant to be shared
To be savored
To be loved
And to be held dearly
The writings are profound
Yet they are so simple
They convey a loving message
Everyone has access
To all the messages
And now this will be
A confirmation
And a renewal
Of all they know

And all they have forgotten
The written word
Is a powerful metaphor
Embracing what is unsaid
And penning it to paper
For all to see
So often
Too much is left unspoken
And it is often in the unspoken
That messages get misinterpreted
Chains of communication
Need to be open
There should be no fear
In opening one's heart
Yet too often
There is fear of reprisal
That people shut down
And do not open themselves
To all that is there for the taking
So many paradoxes abound
You live in a society
Of more opulence and abundance
Of waste and decadence
Yet there is so much
On the flip side
Of a basic need for survival
For living and for roots
For making it through to tomorrow
People who may appear to have it all
May, too, have an emptiness
A bottomless pit
That cannot be

Satiated by having more things
But really needs to be filled
By feeding the soul
Just as poor people are
Starving for food
Too often
People with much wealth
Are starving, too
Yet they are starving for
Meaning in their lives
Finding their real purpose
Making a difference
But there are many
Who are on a roller coaster
Of life
Of going higher and higher
Of seeking more thrills
And greater adventures
Of climbing higher and higher
Up the ladder
To nowhere
They don't know when
To stop the roller coaster
Or how to stop the roller coaster
Yet the hope is
When the roller coaster slows
People will question
People will ponder
People will reflect
And they will find themselves
And they will know themselves
And out of this

Will emerge the goodness
And kindness of the spirit
Of giving rather than receiving
Of sharing the abundance
Of selflessness not selfishness
Of helping with a joyful heart
The time is now
For people to stop the roller coaster
And to experience
Adventures they never envisioned
Making their hearts full
Knowing their life's purpose
No longer will they be empty
No longer will they question
The answers are all within
Waiting to be shared
In a beautiful tomorrow
There is hope and faith
That tomorrow will be full

There is no right way
There is no wrong way
There is only the way
That is right
For each individual

WHO ARE WE?

The question
Should be
Who are we?
We are a culmination
Of knowledge
Of wisdom
Of thought
We are a continuum
Of love
Of light
Of peace
We are teachers
We are mothers
We are fathers
We are rich people
We are poor people
We are every person
We are Guides
Who now know
Who now understand
Who want to share
And pass this wisdom
To all those
Ready to share
We are a team
Working together
We are here
To support you
To nurture you
We are here

EVERYTHING IS FOR A REASON

The task you have set
Will be a metaphor for life
There will be days
Of clear sailing
Yet on other days
There will be choppy waters
Some things will come
With pure ease
Yet there will be
Challenges, hurdles and obstacles
To overcome
Remember everything is for a reason
The obstacles have their due course
And keep you on course
To navigate the water
Even though you think
You are on course
The detours are needed
To steer you where
You need to go
With the flow of the tides
To stay on the course
As best as you can
But to understand
There will be rough water days
And to find ways and means
To navigate those days
The sailboat starts in one place
And has a finish point

Sometimes that boat
Steers slightly off course
As the winds of change
Steer it another direction
So, too, may you be
Steered in an alternative direction
However, it is the journey
And the trip the sailboat takes
That is the essence of being
In the sailboat
And so it is with this task
Writing and compiling
You are the writer
You are the captain of the ship
Steering it this way and that
We are the winds to guide you
We are the water to support you
We are the sun to warm you
We are the clouds to protect you
We will help you navigate the way
But you will always be the captain
You are the one to open your heart
You have the key to the ship
The ship is at a standstill
Without the key being turned
So, too, is it with your writing
Whenever you are ready
To open your heart
To writing the words
We will be your ship
We will anchor you
When you need

We will cruise with you
When you need
We will go into high gear
When you need
You have all the controls
You need to steer the ship
Into beautiful sunsets
And beautiful dawns
You are the navigator
You are the adventurer
You are the captain
At times you will traverse
Unchartered territories
And make remarkable discoveries
At times you will traverse
Discovered lands
It is all part of the process
Of discovery
So as you continue your voyage
Know that there are
Ebbs and flows in the water
The currents will carry you
Through peaceful and turbulent water
Anytime you want
You can anchor the ship
And stop for a while
To reflect
To absorb
To ponder
The journey you have taken
Thus far

LOVE AND FAITH

The universal topics
Of love and faith
Are the ones
That unite all others
With love and faith
There is unity
There is connection
There are no divides
With love and faith
All is possible
It all starts
With love of self
By loving oneself
One is able to extend
And love others
To reach out
And love all that abounds
In the universe
In nature
In the world
But first there must be love of self
Acceptance of self
Loving kindness to self
Nurturing of self
Caring for self
Taking care of self
Blessing and loving self
Each and every day

Only by loving self
Can one then reach out
And love others
You are the start
Of where it all begins
Each person loving
In the highest way
Will give way
To these people
Being able to take that love
And radiate it outwards
Each person
Radiating that self-love
To the outside
Will result
In a loving and peaceful world
Always there must first
Be self-love
By each person
Then there must be faith
Knowing, trusting, believing
Once one has self-love
Faith will be a natural progression
People will believe
And trust
And know
Love and faith
Go hand in hand
It is so simple
And everything is possible
And attainable

With love and faith
All the topics
Flow from love and faith
Work in harmony
When there is love and faith
Anything and everything is possible
Where there is love and faith
Always remember
You are loved
You carry the love
You spread the love
You radiate the love
And the love is returned to you
A circle of love
Continues and continues
Yet when the cycle of love
Is broken
This is when
Self-love is most needed
To going back to the beginning
And loving oneself
For it is only by loving oneself
One can love out of oneself
And spread the love outwards
When there is lack of self-love
And loathing of self
And criticism of self
And not honoring of self
It is not possible to come
From a loving place
And spread love

So foremost
Is the topic of love
Without love
There would be no purpose
Life is love
Love is life

Always remember
You are loved
You carry the love
You spread the love
You radiate the love
And the love is returned to you

CIRCLES OF LOVE

Love is at the center
Of every circle
Love is a gentle unfolding
Of feelings
Of thoughts
Of knowing
Love is round
It goes in a circle
Starting at the center
With self
And self-love
The circle widens and expands
As the love
Radiates outward
And grows and grows
The more one loves
The greater the circle grows
The capacity of love is endless
The size of the circle unlimited
The circles of love
Intercept and meet
At different times
And in different places
Within the circle
The more circles there are
The more there is love
Yet always at each center
There is self-love

Sometimes the circles
Are very small
And hardly apparent
Due to the lack of self-love
Other circles are so vast
And meet with many circles
Of different sizes
The greater the love of self
The greater the power
To spread the love
To share the love
And in turn to feel the love returned
Imagine all the circles
Of love
Waiting to be shared
It all starts with self-love
At the center
Then spreads out
Casting a wider rim
The more one loves
The greater the circle grows
And so it perpetuates itself
Growing and growing
As more love
Enters the circle
A mother with a newborn
Shows how the circle grows
The newborn gives love
And the love is returned
And so develops
A mother's love

Growing and growing
As the love develops
Love is never static
It is in constant flow
There is an elasticity
A flexibility
Pulling this way and
Then the other way
Love has the capacity
To expand in an
Unlimited way
But on the flip side
Love has the ability
To constrict
To retract
To tighten
Forcing the circles to diminish
To shrink
And sometimes cease to be
So circles of love
Meet and intercept
And love is shared
Sometimes the meeting
Of the circles takes place
Within different parts of the circle
And the place of meeting
Is not the same
And so people have
Different expectations
Of the love
They are receiving

And of the love
They are giving
It all depends
On where in each circle
The other circle meets
The nearer to the center
The closer the connection
Yet one circle can meet
Close to one circle
Yet be at the perimeter
Of another circle
Leading to unrequited love
So where the circles meet
Determines the love
That will develop
And whether the love will grow
Love is never static
The circles move and grow
Each person's circle
Moving individually
Yet together with
All the other circles
So the circles change
And the loves within
The circle
Adapt and flow
With the changes
Leading to different
Feelings of love
And determining
Whether the love will grow

Or the love will restrict
Love is always a circle
With you at the center
It all begins with you
Loving yourself first
And then radiating
The love outwards
Love is a circle
Love is a chain of circles
Love is round

Love is a gentle unfolding
Of feelings
Of thoughts
Of knowing

GRATITUDE

A closed book
Has many pages
First the book
Needs to be opened
And read
One page at a time
The story unfolding
As the pages are turned
Each page
Leading to the next page
Each chapter
Following the last chapter
The story builds and grows
Around the previous pages
Yet there are still pages
To be read in the book
Pages to be turned
Pages to be absorbed
One reads a book
Turning the pages
One at a time
Absorbing the book
Reflecting on the book
And the book continues
To the final chapter
To the end
But is that the end of the book
Or do you carry the book within

Remembering characters
Reminiscing on scenes
Certain parts of a book
Are forever
Yet each page on its own
Not embedded in the story
Is meaningless
So too is it with gratitude
It starts as a closed book
Once the book is opened
Or the thanks given
The pages turned
The thanks continue
And there is a growing appreciation
Knowing that the appreciation
Will continue into future chapters
Spilling onto the next page
Just as the words are written
Each word building on the previous
And serving as a foundation
For the words to follow
So too is gratitude
A foundation for more
Good things to follow
Each time thanks are given
They serve as a building block
For more thanks
The more one shows appreciation
The more one acknowledges
The gifts one receives
The greater will these gifts be

These need not be

Material gifts

But gifts of one's asking

Each person asking differently

These could be gifts of

Health, prosperity, success

Recognition, achievement

Faith, courage, strength

The list goes on and on

Each person asking for their own gifts

Receiving the gifts

Yet there needs to be appreciation

For these gifts to continue to grow

The more one thanks

The more one is grateful

The bigger the circle

Of gratitude grows

It is a self-perpetuating circle

By asking

One receives

By thanking

It grows

So one feels ready to ask again

Receiving again

Thanking again

So the cycle continues

There is a correlation

Between asking, receiving and thanking

They all work together

Hand in hand

If one of the elements is missing

The cycle of gratitude
Will come to a standstill
Yet it is very simple
Thanks
Ask
Receive
Thanks
Ask
Receive
Thanks
And the cycle
Goes on and on

The more one thanks
The more one is grateful
The bigger the circle
Of gratitude grows
It is a self-perpetuating circle

SELF-LOVE

The art of loving oneself
Is a love that is
Kind and graceful
By loving yourself
Unconditionally and
Without judgment
There is only good intent
The very act of self-love
Is in effect very selfless
Because by loving self
The very opposite of
Selfishness occurs
By caring for oneself
One then has the
Energy and resources
To love and care for others
So taking care of self
First and foremost
Is the most unselfish act
One can partake in
Without self-love
There can be no love
To go around
Loving oneself
Is the most primal
Of all survival mechanisms
By loving and protecting oneself
Only then can that love

Spread and radiate outwards
Again the more one
Loves the self
The more love
There is to radiate outwards
However when fear
And doubt and anger
Enter the circle
The self-love
Changes to a different form
The self-love
Needs to come from
A loving place
To enable it to spread
Also the circles it meets
Need to be loving circles
Else there can be no synergy
Self-love comes first
Through loving oneself
One can love others
By loving others
The love is returned
And in effect multiplies
By the more one loves
So the more one loves
The more the love is multiplied
And the love keeps
Growing and growing
And there is more love to give
So in effect
Once one loves oneself

One has love to give
Once one gives love
The love is returned
Manifold over
The more one loves
The greater the love
That comes back
To the one giving the love
So the love is in
A perpetual cycle
An ever-growing circle
Of constant renewal
And growth
And development
Yet it all begins
With loving oneself
With being
Kind and gentle
Caring and compassionate
To oneself
The love one puts into
Love of self
Then has the
Power and strength
To grow outward
And circle wider
And envelope more love
And grow
Be gentle
Be kind
Be caring

Be generous
First to self
And then the love
Will grow and radiate out
Self-love is the most
Basic act of survival
When practiced in a loving way
It is never selfish
But always selfless
As loving oneself
Effectively
Allows one to love others
Effectively
And so the cycle of love
And the circles of love
Can sustain themselves
And grow
Into eternity

Loving oneself
Is the most primal
Of all survival mechanisms

DICHOTOMOUS SOCIETY

You live in a dichotomous society
One of many contradictions
And one of polar opposites
You live in a time
Of peace and war
Of riches and poverty
Of faith and lack of faith
Of health and sickness
You live in a time
Of great change
There is so much good
In the world
Yet the flip side
Is that there is
An element that is not so good
Love of self is lost
And is not replenished
People live in hatred
And fear
And evil overcomes good
In many places
Yet always
There are specks of love
There are moments of joy
And the hope is
That these specks
Will transform into love
Starting at the essence

Starting with one individual
Each individual
Practicing the art of self-love
One moment to the next
Thinking loving thoughts
Feeling loving thoughts
Knowing loving thoughts
It all starts with the
First thought of love
There are no easy answers
There are no quick fixes
As to how each person
Can love themselves
Yet the more
People love themselves
The more the circles of love
Grow and expand
And the hope
Is eternal
That love will always prevail

Yet always
There are specks of love
There are moments of joy
And the hope is
That these specks
Will transform into love

HEALING

Healing begins within
At the very core
At the essence
Of each individual
Each person
Has access
And the resources
To heal themselves
Yet each person
Has the choice
What parts they
Choose to heal
Healing is not always
Physical healing
And may be construed
As not working
When physical healing
Does not occur
Yet healing
May occur at a
Much deeper level
For that individual
And may be the exact healing
Chosen by that individual
On their journey
To heal
Is to make better
To affect a change

To adapt
To grow within
One's circumstances
It is much easier
To see physical healing
Yet healing within
Is more
Life changing
Life altering
Life affirming
To heal from within
Changes everything
As from within
So is it from without
The healing must
First take place
Within the essence
Of each individual
Some people will appear
To be suffering
And experiencing
Great illness
Great pain
Great suffering
Yet many of these people
Are healed within
And are at peace
With who they are
They live with joy
They live with love
They live in the moment

They are healed
As their spirit is healed
They live in the
Present moment
Knowing this is
What is important
They seem to
Transcend the pain
Accept the pain
Embrace the illness
And the pain
And the suffering
For they are healed
They know
They have not forgotten
The importance
Of living in this
Present moment
As fully as possible

*To heal
Is to make better
To affect a change
To adapt
To grow within
One's circumstances*

THE BUTTERFLY

The gateway to suffering
Is sometimes a long road
That appears to have
No end in sight
The road is treacherous
The conditions are bleak
The obstacles plentiful
There appears to be
No end to the suffering
Yet the very obstacles
And the clamoring
Through the obstacles
Over the obstacles
Around the obstacles
Is the very purpose
For the obstacles
They lead to growth
And expansion
Of the human spirit
If life was devoid
Of suffering
There would be no
Opportunity for the spirit
To grow and develop
The analogy has often been made
Of the butterfly
Emerging from the cocoon
The butterfly has to fight

To battle

To work hard

To break through the cocoon

Without this fight

The wings of the butterfly

Needed for it to soar

Do not develop

And grow

The way they need to grow

So, too, is it with

Suffering and obstacles

They give you the

Tools needed

To survive

To thrive

To soar

To fly

In the very way

You were meant to soar

These obstacles

That one resists

In one's suffering

Need to be embraced

Need to be loved

Need to be worked through

For it is the

Very embracing of the suffering

That leads to growth

And out of the suffering

Shall emerge

All that was intended

Do not fight the obstacles
Do not resist the obstacles
Do not complain
The obstacles
Are the path
To the future
And at times
You may not understand
The reason
The purpose
And why it is so hard
You need to trust
To have faith
To believe
That all will unfold
In a way
That helps to
Keep you on the path
And lead you
Through the passageway
To a better tomorrow

If life was devoid
Of suffering
There would be no
Opportunity for the spirit
To grow and develop

FAITH

Faith is a knowing
An unfaltering belief
A core value
That one intrinsically
Feels
Knows
Believes to be right
Faith is a deep
Unwavering knowing
An unquestionable fact
A solid belief
That everything
Is exactly as it should be
Faith is unfaltering
Yet does bend with the wind
As do the branches of the tree
Faith sways
Back and forth
Yet always
The core is strong
The foundation secure
The knowing intact
That faith is the essence
The circle of faith
A key to the circle of love
They are interchangeable
Faith and love
Are the cornerstones

Of a life

Filled with purpose

Filled with hope

Filled to the brim

With fulfillment

Faith is the unspoken word

It is the silent partner

It is there

Yet it is not there

It is the foundation

Yet it cannot be

Seen

Touched

Felt

Faith is knowing

Believing

Faith embodies everything

By believing

By trusting

By knowing

One knows

Without a doubt

That all is as it

Should be

Faith means different things

To different people

Is experienced in different ways

Is felt in different ways

Is known in different ways

Yet each person believing

In the powers that be

Trusting in their belief system
Knowing
That faith will guide them
Steer them
Support them
Is what is important
Faith begins within
And as the seed
Is planted and grows
And sprouts and develops
So, too, does faith grow
One moment of faith
Unfolding into the next
And so the foundation
Of faith grows
And builds
Within each person
Each person
Housing their own faith
Each person
Having the foundation of their faith
Yet faith on its own
Is not as strong
As faith in unity
So the more people believe
The stronger faith grows
Faith has been known
To move mountains
Faith is solid
Faith is strong
Faith is unwavering

Yet faith is never
At the detriment of another
Faith like love
Is gentle
Is kind
Is compassionate
Faith is
Like a river
That flows
Gently
Moving along the landscape
At times it crosses
Rocky terrain
And the river flows faster
Like a cascading waterfall
Barreling to the bottom
The river does not think
Or know where it will end
Yet the river keeps flowing
Through peaks and valleys
So, too, is it with faith
At times
The path will be gentle
And life will seem to plod along
At an even pace
With no major significance
Then along comes an incident
To test one's faith
To challenge one's belief system
To question the status quo
At these times

It would be easy to give up faith

To not believe

To not trust

To doubt

To question

Yet it is at these very crossroads

That faith

Has the opportunity

To grow

To thrive

To develop

As out of the darkness

Will come the light

Out of suffering

Will emerge hope

Out of the tragedy

Will a new tomorrow prevail

Sunrise always

Follows sunset

Light always

Follows dark

Faith is knowing

Faith is believing

Faith is

Faith and love
Are the cornerstones
Of a life
Filled with purpose

GIVING

The story of Adam
Given the apple
Seems to be the
Beginning of giving
Adam was given an apple
With an open heart
And so the apple
In essence
Becomes the core
Or the metaphor for giving
The gift of giving
Is more in the giving
Than in the gift
It is the positive thought
The energy transmitted
Of giving to another person
It is self-love at a high level
As by giving
One receives
But first one needs self-love
And faith
That one has all one needs
So they can give
And the cycle
Or the circle
Of giving
And receiving
Continues

And perpetuates itself
Giving from the heart
Giving of oneself
Giving one's love
Giving unconditionally
With no expectations
Leads to bigger returns
As giving
Is ultimately getting
As one gives
So shall one receive
And the exchange
Takes place
It is a circle
One does the asking
One receives
One thanks
And giving completes the circle
As when one asks
Another needs to give
In order for one to receive
Yet the giver
Who is giving
Is also receiving
As to give
Is to receive
The more one gives
The more one receives
The greater the circle grows
And the more one
Wants to give

Yet there are many
Who choose not to give
Or choose to give
Only things
They fear that if they give
They will not have enough
Or that they will
Not get back
Yet there is so much abundance
And the more one gives
The more one is able to give
The more it comes back
There needs to be faith
There needs to be trust
And always an open heart
Knowing
Trusting
Believing
Giving is receiving
There is joy in receiving
The circle
Of giving grows
With gratitude
As the giver
Too, receives

CHOICE

Life is a series of passages
Of doorways
That are opened and closed
The choice is always yours
Of whether to enter
Or bypass the doorway
At times the choices
Are clear
And it is easy
To enter the doorway
And navigate the passage
Other times
The choices are not so easy
As to whether
To enter or bypass the door
To explore the passage
Beyond the door
The choice may be easier
Not to enter the door
Not to enter the unknown
Yet it is by no means
Always the best choice
Walking the passage
To the yet unopened door
Often leads to
New challenges
Growth
Development

To new experiences
And adventures
Which would not have been experienced
Encountered and lived
Had that door not been opened
And the passageway explored
To open
Or not to open
And how far
To walk through the doorway
Are always
Personal choices to be made
Trust needs to be invoked
Decisions wrestled with
The scales go back and forth
As to whether to
Enter or not
The choice is yours
For many passages
Yet other passages
Will not be ones of your choosing
These could be thrust upon you
Or happen in a gradual way
Over time
There is always one constant
Life is never static
Change is a constant
Fact of life
And it is the ability
To be able to bend with the changes
That helps to navigate

The passages in an easier manner
Resistance always makes the journey
More difficult
More cumbersome
And harder than it needs to be
Knowing where to go with the flow
Knowing when to proceed
And knowing when to stop
Are key elements
In exploring the passages
You will surely encounter
As you travel
On the journey
Of loving
Of living
Of being

Life is never static
Change is a constant
Fact of life
And it is the ability
To be able to bend with the changes
That helps to navigate
The passages in an easier manner

Seasons

Seasons are the
Quadrants by which
Your year is divided
A time to rest
A time to grow
A time to be
A time to change
Yet within each season
There is always change
As is there always rest, being and growth
The cycles of life
Seem to follow a pattern
In nature
The pattern is easy to follow
And is more discernable
Winter follows fall
As surely as summer follows spring
Yet in humankind
The seasons of life
Could take different routes
At different speeds
People progress through their seasons
In their time, space and speed
Many people seem to spend
All their time in winter
Appearing to be resting
And waiting and sleeping
Their days are slow

Their energy low
They have no need
To be anyplace
Or anywhere
But just to rest
This is where they need to be
This is their season
In time they may choose
To move out of winter's comfort
Into the hope of spring
And the growth
That spring inspires
Yet it is all up
To each individual
How they choose
To spend their time
Being attuned to nature
Is often reflected
In the way
People live their lives
They follow the beat of nature
Listening to the sounds
Seeing the sights
That the changes
Of the seasons bring
They live their lives
Harmoniously
Flowing with nature
Flowing with the changes
They, too, take time
To rest

To grow
To be
To change
Time after time
Rest. Grow.
Be. Change.
All the way to eternity

The cycles of life
Seem to follow a pattern
In nature
The pattern is easy to follow

LIVE IN THIS MOMENT

Live each day
In splendor
For there is
Much to behold
Live each day
In this moment
For it is in the moment
That life
Is truly lived
Love each moment
Spread the love
Feel the love
Loving is giving
Giving is loving
Remember to love self
Each and every day
Nurture yourself
Support yourself
Compassion and caring
Of yourself
Feeling self-love
Leads to abundance
The circles will grow
The circles will connect
Live in this moment
Live in love
Spread the love

HOPE

Hope is a journey
Into an enchanted tomorrow
Hope is a dream
For a better tomorrow
Hope is a wish
Hope is a desire
Hope is a longing
That all will be well
Hope is a means of asking
Yet it is not asking
Hope is a possibility
Hope needs to be tied to faith
Connected to faith
Hope needs to be believed
Too often hope is ethereal
It is not real
Or the hoping
Is not stated
In a real context
So hope's dreams
Are difficult to interpret
As they are not understood
One needs to believe
One needs faith
And a vision
Of what they hope for
Too often
Hope is not real

For the person doing the hoping
They hope
Yet they do not really believe
In the true possibilities
Of what hoping can bestow
They have doubts
And justifications
As to why
Hoping is dreaming
And that what they
Hope
Cannot become
What they want
Too often
They do not know
What it is they want
Thus, in effect
They cannot get
What they really do not know
They think they hoped for
One needs to ask
For what one needs
Only then
Can one get
What was asked for
Hoping is not a solid belief
Hoping is a maybe
Hoping is vague
One needs to believe
To visualize
To experience

In as much detail
As possible
What one wants
Before it can be manifested
One needs to be specific
In what one requests
To be able to receive
What one wants
Hoping is too general
Hoping is too vague
Hoping is too non-descript
Know what it is you want
Ask for what you want
Transform hope into desire
By being specific
Ask
Receive
Thanks
It is an ever-enduring circle
That is self-sustaining
And ever-growing
Hope is but a step
In the process
Yet hope
Needs to be elevated
To the next step
To asking
Else hope
Often remains
A step that is not transcended
To the next step

Of asking
Leading to the next step
Of receiving
And onto the next step
Of thanking
So hope is part of the process
Yet only one step
Of the process
Too often
Hope remains as hope
As the next steps
Are not taken
To complete the cycle

Hope is a journey
Into an enchanted tomorrow
Hope is a dream
For a better tomorrow

WITHIN THE SELF

You live in a world of change
Of progress
Of technology
Of advancement
Of striving
Everything moves at the
Speed of light
Today's inventions
Will be tomorrow's desires
The world you live in
Moves so quickly
People do not take the time
To stop
To think
To reflect
As they are too busy
Clamoring to stay
With the status quo
Of how they believe
They should live their lives
They do not take the time
To go within
To be still
To be quiet
All the answers
To all life's questions
Are within
Each individual
Yet most people
Are able to connect

At all levels
With different people
Fast changing technology
Yet are unable and
Unwilling to take time
To connect within
To know oneself
They are too busy
Connecting without themselves
So being without
They cannot be within
Where all the basic answers
To life's greatest questions
Are to be found
Not living within
Leads to a life
Without purpose
Without fulfillment
Without knowing
Yet people
Do not understand
That it all begins
Within the self
Within each individual
There is the capacity
To know everything
One needs to know
One just needs to go within
To access the answer
Else one will be without
The choice is up to you

WE ARE ALL LIGHT

The light shines
All around you
A circle of light
A circle of energy
It protects you
It surrounds you
It supports you
The circle is a true metaphor
That everything goes round
There is no beginning
And there is no end
To the circle
It is round
The circle has no clear start
And no definite destination
It keeps going
Round and round
So too life is a circle
It moves within the circle
At different levels
Within the circle
At times you will live
Within the inner sanctums
Of your circle
At times you will
Reach outwards
Extending your circle
Reaching outwards

And embracing
Other circles
We are all circles
We are all light
We are all energy
We all have the capacity
To grow our circles
To connect
To be one
With the universe
The power of one circle
Meeting another circle
Leads to greater
Love
Energy
Peace
So the more the circles meet
The greater the good
That will prevail
As always it all begins
With self-love
And taking care of self
The love will spread
The love will radiate
The love will grow
Inward and outward
Round and round
There is no beginning
There is no end
There is plenty of light
There is ample love

There is much abundance
To be shared
And to be known

The light shines
All around you
A circle of light
A circle of energy
It protects you
It surrounds you
It supports you

INNER VOICE

The center is where it all begins
The center of the circle
Initiating with self-love
Taking care of self
First and foremost
Loving oneself
Knowing oneself
Is the ultimate in self-care
By listening to the inner voice
Stirring within
One needs to validate that voice
And take action
So it is paramount
To take time for self
To quieten down
To stop doing
To listen
And to hear
To acknowledge
To feel
To validate
To respect
Those inner voices
Listen to the advice
Practice the art of listening
For all the answers
Are within
For you to hear

Too often
One jumps on the
Wheels of life
And the circle keeps
Turning and turning
Faster and faster
It is hard to stop the wheel
That is in constant motion
Yet you need
To apply the brakes
Put out the stops
To stop the circle
And go back to
The center of the circle
The self-love needs
To be constantly replenished
Self needs to be nurtured
With compassion
Loving kindness
Peace and harmony
For out of the stillness
The answers you seek
Are waiting
To be heard by you
Yet sometimes it is easier
To keep going
With the wheels that
Are already in motion
It takes courage
It takes thought
It takes foresight

To stop the wheel
And in essence
To recharge the essence
Which is self
The wheel will keep running
Until it hits a roadblock
Or runs out of air
Taking care of the wheel
Along the journey
Will ensure a safer journey
As you will have
Listened to your inner voice
And know the answers
Assisting you to find balance
By nurturing your center
And you are always
At the center
Of your circle
When you take self-care
However when self-care
Steps are not taken
You move out of the center
Of the circle
And the wheel tilts
And does not run smoothly
So it is important
To stay within your center
So the circle can
Keep turning
At the pace you set
Keep growing

At the pace you love
Take care of self
And you will
Feel more centered
More balanced
More energized
Be quiet
Be still
Listen
The answers are within

Practice the art of listening
For all the answers
Are within
For you to hear

BELIEVE

First one has to ask
Before one can receive
Ask the question
Let it "Be"
"Lieve" the question
And Believe it will be
Trust it will be
Ask – Be – Leave
And so it shall come to pass
You will receive
You will believe
You will give thanks
And the cycle will continue

Trust it will be
Ask – Be – Leave
And so it shall come to pass

BEING IN THE MOMENT

Relax into this moment
For it is here
And then it is gone
To be present in the moment
Is the greatest gift
Or present
You can give
By being in the moment
You get
Yet you also receive
You are present
You are flowing
You do not resist
Being present
Being in the moment
Is the greatest gift
For too often
People dwell in lost yesterdays
And missed opportunities
Their present of yesterday
Is their past of today
That present
Could have been their gift
To themselves
And to the world
So it is paramount
To always be in the present
To savor the moment

To not rush time

To believe in tomorrow

Yet not to the detriment

Of missing out on today

Living in the now

Is the greatest gift

You can bestow

Being present

Being open

Being aware

Listening with an open heart

With no judgment

With no motives

Leads to the greatest present

Serving as a foundation

For a solid tomorrow

The present

Is a building block

And the more

You build the blocks

Of your current present

The greater will the foundation

Be for the future

You believe

Yet it all starts

With the present moment

Being in this moment

Living this moment fully

Living this moment openly

And with the belief

That all is possible

THE TREASURE BOX

Listening is an art form
Too many have lost
The silence is maddening
And the void it creates
Feels empty to them
So the silence
Is filled with
Noise
Yet too often
The noise is empty
The noise is meaningless
There is no value
In the noise
Yet often the noise
Fills a void
A vacuum
A space
That the individual
Does not trust
To enter
The empty space
Or the silence
Is the place
Where all the answers reside
The quiet
The stillness
The solitude
Need to be felt

Need to be encountered
Need to be absorbed
As by being still and silent
One will be within
One can listen
To one's inner voice
To one's inner longings
To one's inner knowing
The space feeling empty
The silent space
Is truly a treasure chest
Of the finest gems
And diamonds
One could ever hope
To excavate
In the red of rubies
One will find love
In the clearness of diamonds
One will find clarity
In the white of pearls
Will wisdom be found
The treasures are all there
You have the key
To unlock the treasures
The potential is unlimited
The treasure box overflowing
With everything you need
By accessing the treasures
Or by being silent
And listening
By going within

And not always
Filling your life
With meaningless chatter
The journey of discovery
Will take you
On a journey of awakening
Of knowing
You will find the answers
All the finest gems
In the world
Are within
Take time to be still
Take time to stop
Take time to listen
And you will flow
As all is revealed
To you
Layer by layer
Gently unfolding
As you give it time
The answers will
Present to you
Be still
Be quiet
Listen

You have the key
To unlock the treasures

BALANCE

The stillness of the night
Gives way
To the noise of the day
Darkness becomes light
Quiet turns to sound
They balance each other
Like weights on a scale
Peace and harmony
Tipping the scale
In one direction
War and discord
Countering the scale
In another direction
Finding the center
Finding the balance
Finding the core
A balancing act
To find one's center
Some people gravitate
To a center of peace
Yet other people
Gravitate towards discord
Each person's center
Their own to claim
Their own to find
Their own to balance
The scales work together
Towards balance
Towards equilibrium

Towards the center
Yet there are always
Opposing forces
Pulling in opposite directions
Tipping the scales
This way and that way
You need to find the center
You need to find your center
The center is unique to you
It is your equilibrium
It is your balance
It is your core
Finding your center
Honoring your center
Loving your center
Will enable you to
Radiate from within your center
And grow your circle
Outward
Upward
And beyond
Yet first and foremost
You need to find your center

You need to find your center
The center is unique to you
It is your equilibrium
It is your balance
It is your core

THE SURFER

The waves ebb and flow
Cresting at the top of the wave
The foaming water
White and frothy
Camouflaging the clear
Waters beneath the surface
The surfer rides the waves
Anticipating
Waiting
Beckoning
Riding what he believes
To be the perfect wave
Skimming over the crest of the wave
Moving in unison with the wave
Through the wave
Through the froth
Emerging through the wave
And gliding into the clear water
So too does it seem
That the journey
Is not always clear
Yet one needs to ride the waves
At times the surfer
Will fall from his surfboard
And be tossed
And turned in the waves
Yet the surfer will emerge
Only to once again

Embark on the journey
To find the perfect wave
To ride with the ebb and the flow
Of the calm waters
And the crashing waves
Not every wave is perfect
Not every ride complete
Yet the surfer
Continues his quest
To keep surfing
There is oft failure
When the surfer falls
When the surfer stumbles
When the surfer crashes
Into the rumbling waves
Yet the surfer
Believes
Knows
Wants the next wave
To be the one he catches
The surfer does not give up
Intuitively
Knowingly
With true belief
The surfer keeps going
Riding the waves
Catching the waves
There is a sense of failure
When the surfer falls
Yet the true sign of success
Is that the surfer

Chooses to ride

Again and again

Again and again

Despite falling

Despite crashing

Despite the fear

The surfer chooses

To ride

One wave after another

Always believing

The chosen wave

Is the perfect one

Yet many times

The wave crashes

Into the surfer

And the surfer

Must battle to emerge

Through the froth

And the power

Of the wave

To survive

The wrath of the water

The waves ebb and flow

One wave following the other

The surfer is patient

The surfer keeps watch

For what he believes

To be the perfect wave

Moving fluidly in the wave

Uniting with the wave

Moving with the changes

The wave travels
The surfer and the wave
Are one
Are united
Are together
Cruising to the end of the wave
The surfer returns
To the waves and the water
To wait for the next wave
And so it goes
Onward and upward
One ride following the next
Not every ride perfect
Yet the surfer
Believes and knows
That the next wave
Could be the perfect wave
So he keeps embarking
On his surfboard
Waiting for that euphoric feeling
Of being one with the wave
Or being one with the universe
Of flowing effortlessly
With the ebb and flow of the waves
And so it is with life
There are ebbs and flows
In the journey one travels
At times life is filled with euphoria
With good times
And life seems to flow
Effortlessly along

Yet at times there is an ebbing
And the journey is more difficult
Like the surfer
One needs to keep going
Believing
Knowing
That the waves will continue
To ebb and flow
So from the ebb
Eventually will the flow emerge
And the next wave
Could be the perfect wave

And so it is with life
There are ebbs and flows
In the journey one travels

TRAIN OF LIFE

The tracks of the train
Run parallel
The distance between them
Always the same
There is no deviation
From one place to the next
Enabling the train to
Stay on course
And not be derailed
If the tracks were uneven
The train could not
Follow the course
Stay the distance
Reach its destination
Engineers measure the course
Every inch of the way
Ensuring the train
Is able to follow the route
It was meant to travel
The railroad tracks
Are set in place
Allowing the train
To run its course
So too is your life
Destined to run its course
The tracks have been laid
Allowing you to travel
From one destination

To the next
At times the train
Will stop
And you will disembark
At the station
Each station
Will have
What you need at that time
And you will stay
At that station
Until you are ready
To resume your journey
You will bypass
Some stations
And there will be other stations
Which you will revisit
As each station
On the journey
Is part of the path
You have chosen to travel
Each station
Offers different lessons
Has different messages
For it is a
Train of life
That travels the course
Predestined for you
You have the ticket
To ride the train
Whenever you choose
It is an open ticket

With no restrictions
You are the one
Who makes the choices
Of where to travel
And where to stop
The train is always ready
To travel
The distance with you
For it is a train of life
And you are
The conductor

Each station
Offers different lessons
Has different messages
For it is a
Train of life
That travels the course
Predestined for you

SILENCE

Be silent
Be still
Be quiet
The voice within
Talks in whispers
Needing silence
To be heard
Too often
The noise of the day
Blocks out
The quiet of the inner voice
By being still
By being quiet
Only then can one
Truly be
For it is in the silence
That being becomes possible
Turn off the noise
Turn off the chaos
Switching to quiet
Turns up the inner voice
Waiting to be heard
For it is from within
That your true self
Resides
And patiently waits
To be heard
For you to listen
For you to be

THERE IS ALWAYS FLOW

Gently the breeze blows
Bringing relief
To the still air
The movement of the wind
Follows a path
There is no stopping
The direction of the wind
For it moves
As it is meant to move
The wind moves through valleys
And over mountains
There is no stopping
The path of the wind
At times the wind speed
May increase
And become faster
Yet at times the speed
Seems to halt
Yet always there are currents flowing
And movement
There is always flow
There is always change
As the natural elements
Flow in harmony
One season following
The season that came before
At times it seems
As though there is no change

From one day to the next
Yet slowly
An indiscernible change
Takes place
And the next season
Flows into place
For the seasons
Are meant to be
Although the changes are slight
From day to day
Over the course of weeks
The changes do occur
And slowly the winter
Gives way to spring
And growth occurs
Where there had been no growth
For the changing of the seasons
Heralds in a new today
A day filled with promise
A day filled with hope
For the present
Is truly the gift
Of a complete tomorrow

THE STAIRCASE

The wisdom of the ages
Has been known to many
The sages and guides
Documenting and recording
The treasure cove of information
Sharing the knowledge
Beholding the truth
Opening the way
So the masses will know
How to unlock the wisdom
To turn the key
Opening the door
To lead them into awareness
And understanding
Too often the door is locked
And people are barred from entering
Yet once the key has been turned
There is no retreating
As the door has been opened
To a fresh start
Of learning and exploring
Beyond the door
Is a stairway of learning
Each step serving as
The stepping stone
To more knowledge
And more depth
It is truly an oxymoron

As the higher up the staircase
One travels
The deeper the wisdom
And understanding
That one acquires
The steps are not meant
For sprinting
But rather should be taken
At a slower pace
Giving time to absorb
The lessons in each step
To understand
To grasp
To experience
The newfound knowledge
Each will acquire
As one ascends the steps
Each person
Will have their own stairway
Unique to the path
They have chosen to travel
So the series of steps
Is individually tailored
Depending on the journey
Of the individual
Each step
A stepping stone
And foundation
For the next step
No two steps the same
In the journey

The staircase is unlike
Any you have seen
Some steps are small and short
While others have a long
Vertical leap
To reach the next level
There are twists and curves
In the stairway
And sometimes within the stairway
There will be descending steps
One will encounter
All part of the journey
To knowing oneself
To find oneself
To being
To be

Each person
Will have their own stairway
Unique to the path
They have chosen to travel

THE MELODY

The tone has been set
The instrument tuned
For the melody
That will surely follow
Each instrument in accord
With the tune to be played
The musicians knowing their pieces
Having practiced
To perfect the notes
The harmony resounding
Through the cumulative sounds
Of the individual instruments
Each note of music
Beautiful on its own
Yet it is in the unity
Of the instruments
That the true splendor
And the melodic sounds
Of the combined notes
Leads to a rhapsody
Combining the different sounds
In true harmony
Each musician knows his place
In performing
In playing
In flowing with the music
For they are in sync
With joining together

To create a melody

Each musical instrument

Vital to the tune

Each instrument

Providing a different element

A different sound

Each instrument

Unique to itself

Yet together the instruments

Blend and unite

Creating sounds

That in their combination

And unity

Transcend

The sounds of only one instrument

And so it is with life

Each person

Playing their own tune

Each person

Having their own role

There is true beauty

In each individual

And every person

Has their notes to play

Yet it is the unity

Of individuals

Playing together

Living together

Joining together

That leads to perfect harmony

GROWTH

A clear day beckons
The sky a pure blue
No clouds in sight
A picture perfect day
The sunshine warms the fields
Nurturing the plants
Calling on them
To start the growing process
Winter's demise
Leading to spring
And the process of growth
The flowers soon to bloom
Yet for now
Are still in the growth phase
For though we cannot see the flowers
The process of awakening
And the work of growing
Happens
Beyond what we can see
Slowly the blooms will appear
Ready to flower
When the time is right
The plants continually grow
Yet they too
Have a time to rest
The stark days of winter
Providing the plants
With the conditions to go within

Back to the beginning
To being a seed
And going through the growth process
Year after year
Time after time
The seasons change
Yet the cycle continues
Of growth and renewal

The process of awakening
And the work of growing
Happens
Beyond what we can see

THE PATH

The cobbled stones
Line the path
In a haphazard manner
There is no set pattern
In the cobbled stones
Yet stepping from one stone
To the next stone
Leads one along the path
To the destination
Of where the path leads
Some of the stones
Are smooth and pleasing
To the eye
Whilst other stones
Are rough and have
A mottled appearance
There are big stones
And small stones
That one will encounter
On the journey
Yet each stone
Needs to be traversed
Along the path
One is traveling
Some stones are set off
From the path
And may appear
As a detour

On the journey
Yet they are part of the path
Stepping from stone to stone
Can be compared
To skipping from one
Experience to the next
Each experience in life
Serving as a stepping stone
To the next experience
No two stones alike
As are no two experiences
The same
They may look the same
They may feel the same
Yet there are unique differences
In the way
One experiences life's teachings
Two people encountering
The exact same experience
Will feel different emotions
Depending upon where they
Are in their journey of life
And what experiences
They have previously lived
Many teachings discuss
The open mind and
The open heart
Yet the human condition
And the thoughts one harbors
Affect the experiences
One lives

Through the practice of stillness
Of being silent
Of retreating within
The possibility of being open
Receptive
Clear
And awake
Becomes a reality
And there is clarity
In one's thoughts
For within the stillness
And within the silence
The essence of who
You are within
Will be known to you
And as you encounter
The cobbled steps
Along your journey
You will trust
You will know
That the path you travel
Is the path
You are destined to follow

Each experience in life
Serving as a stepping stone
To the next experience

BE STILL

At day's end
When darkness enters
And night falls
When the flurry of activities subside
This is the time to be
To be still
As one goes to sleep
And the plethora
Of daily duties ends
Often signals the time to be awake
For in sleep
We are within
We are quiet
We are still
There are no disturbances
And we are free
To be
Who we truly are
So paradoxically
When we are asleep
We are awake
And when we are awake
We are asleep
And the cycle
Repeats itself
Day after day
Yet many now
Want to remain awake

For as the dawn breaks
And the light enters
There is a desire
There is a longing
There is a need
To better understand
The realm of the universe
To know oneself
And to be
One with self

When we are asleep
We are awake
And when we are awake
We are asleep

SOLITUDE

The solitude of the moment
A gift to behold
For this time
Of stillness
Of quietness
Is the time
To go within
For within the solitude
Within the core
Within the center
Is the essence
Of who you really are
Within this quiet center
Are the answers
To all your questions
Within your center
Lies your inner wisdom
Accessible to you
At any time
Taking the time
To be still
To be quiet
To be content
To be grateful
To go within
Leads you to the answers
You seek
For you have

All the answers
They are the core
Of who you are
They are the essence
Of who you are
They are the center
Of who you are
Within the moment of solitude
By going within
You will know
All you need to know

For within the solitude
Within the core
Within the center
Is the essence
Of who you really are

GRATEFUL HEART

A grateful heart
Is open to receiving
As by acknowledging
That which is received
It reinforces
The cycle of asking
And receiving
The simple act of gratitude
Of being thankful
Of being grateful
Of being appreciative
Confirms the receipt
Of that which was asked
And perpetuates the cycle
Of asking
And receiving

SPRING

Spring is beckoning
As the days get longer
And the air warmer
The cold days of winter
Replaced by warmth and growth
For spring is a season
Of rejuvenation
Of growth
Of experimenting
It is a new season
After the dormant days of winter
The crisp air of spring
Feels good to the body
Yet it is the mind
That is truly beckoned by spring
The mind awakens
It has been replenished
From winter's slumber
And awakens to the possibilities
Available to the living
Of being alive
Of being unlimited
Of being receptive
And open
To the joy of being
Spring is a time of growth
A time to bloom
A time to blossom

A time of renewal
For within the promise of spring
Lies the potential
For fulfillment
Of oneself

For spring is a season
Of rejuvenation
Of growth
Of experimenting
It is a new season

THE BELLS

The bells toll in the distance
Resounding one after the other
Each sound replaced by the next
Yet merging
In time and space
The bells echo
In the distance
Rhythmic, melodic
Systematically
One chime following the next
Until the last chime
Is replaced by silence
For awhile
Yet one knows
The bells will toll again
On time
In unison
Together

MOVE WITH THE FLOW

As you embark
On your journey
Of discovering yourself
Of knowing yourself
There will be many stops
And destinations to explore
At times the journey
Will unravel effortlessly
And you will move
Through the flow
With the flow
And be in the present moment
Absorbing the moment
Experiencing the moment
Learning from the moment
For when you move with the flow
There is no resistance
There is no fear
There are no doubts
Allowing your journey
To go in the direction
You need it to go
By being open
By being receptive
By trusting
The flow will continue
Be open to the possibilities
For they abound

All around you
Waiting for you
To open your eyes
To open your heart
To open your mind
To the vast expanse
And the unlimited opportunities
That await you
Yet too often
You live in a state of doubt
Blocking the flow
Blocking the opportunities
And closing the door
To all that lies beyond
You live in a time
Where much is questioned
Yet you live in a time
Where you know the answers
For this is a time
To be
All you need to be

Be open to the possibilities
For they abound
All around you

THE SPARROW

The song of the sparrow
Echoes in the distance
A call to action
A call to join
The sparrow sings
A song of joy
Inviting other birds
To join the melody
For spring is here
The warm weather beckons
After winter's respite
For spring signals growth
And expansion
All that lay dormant
Now ready to emerge
The time is right
The conditions are aligned
For all living things
To grow
To develop
To be full
For spring is a time
Of energy
Of renewal
Of excitement
Of promise
Of potential
Spring offers hope
Eternal
A time to start anew

A time for creation
A time of being
A time to be
The winds of change
Blowing peacefully
Through the air
Inspiring a call to action
The cold days of winter
Replaced by
The warmer days of spring
Enticing one to step outside
To be one with nature
To experience the elements
By stepping outside
Into the warmth of spring
Awakens the inner you
As you embrace
As you experience
As you grow
In spring's hope
For spring implores growth
Of all living things
Move with the flow
Bend with the changes
Grow with the light
Adapt to the conditions
For as a plant
Grows, survives and thrives
So, too, do you
Grow, survive and thrive
Wherever you are planted

TIME

The hands of the clock
Turn constantly
Showing the hour
The minutes, the seconds
Time is never static
And there is constant flow
Time is but a reflection
Of the way you spend your present
For this moment
And how you live
Within this very moment
And within every moment
Is the basis for the life
You choose to live
Time is always moving
Forward in a methodical way
Yet there are times
When it appears as though
Time is at a standstill
Yet other times
Time moves rapidly
And one wonders
Where the time went
In your lives
Time seems to define
So many different things
And your lives
Are controlled

By the hands of the clock
Too often
How you spend your time
Is due to the time on the clock
Rather than on your
Internal clock
Which moves to the rhythm
And flow of who you are
Yet you rely on
What the clock shows
To determine how to live your life
When to wake
And when to sleep
When to work
And when to play
When to eat
And when to rest
For you live in a world
Obsessed with time
And how to best
Utilize the hours
The days
The weeks
The months
Yet by slowing down
And going within
By living with meaning
And purpose
Within this present moment
The moments that flow
As a result

Of living with intention
Will flow from your center
From the essence
Of who you are
You live in a time
When time defines too much
And too much energy
Is devoted to thoughts of tomorrow
And what the future holds
You need to
Choose to live in this moment
For the time you live
To be enriched
To be meaningful
To be full
It is your time
To live your life
In this present moment

For this moment
And how you live
Within this very moment
And within every moment
Is the basis for the life
You choose to live

THE PENDULUM

The pendulum
Swings back and forth
Across the axis
It swings
Back and forth
The axis is the center
The pendulum traverses
As it flows
Rhythmically back and forth
Hypnotic in its movement
As it moves
This way
And then the other way
The forces working in unison
To keep the momentum
And flow of the pendulum
Opposing forces
Working together
To create the flow
The push and the pull
Working in unity
Blending together
Maintaining the flow
Back and forth
Always crossing the center
Time and time again
Moving away from the center
Moving over the center
Flowing in the alternate direction
And back over the center again

The pendulum moves
And so it is with life
There is always the call
To the center
To the essence
Yet there are forces
That pull and push
One away from the center
And back to the center again
There is constant energy
There is constant movement
There is always a flow
Moving one towards one's center
And then away again
For life is not static
But always flowing
The flow is to the center
Yet forces
Work together
Both in harmony
And in discord
To tilt one off center
For a time
Yet the flow
Will always return
To the center
Back and forth
Over the axis
For forces working together
Flowing across
The center

THE BREATH

The journey to the inner self
Begins with the breath
Inhaling slowly within
Exhaling and releasing
That which does not belong
Letting go of the noise
The judgments
The pandemonium
The thoughts
That clutter our minds
And capture our souls
Breathe
In and out
Breathe
In and out
Slowly returning to the still place
The place of wisdom
Of serenity
Of knowledge
Of peace
This haven of peace
This sanctuary of healing
This garden of love
Readily accessible to you
As you breathe
As you slow down
As you quiet down
And go within

By entering the silence
And being still
Allows one to hear
The inner voice
That too often
Is blocked
By all the noise
Listen to the voice
For within the silence
Are the answers
To all your questions
You ask
As you travel
On your journey
Embrace the silence
Welcome the quiet
For within the stillness
And the solitude
You are home
And you will know
You are home

*By entering the silence
And being still
Allows one to hear
The inner voice
That too often
Is blocked*

TRUST WHAT YOU KNOW

The joy is immense

There is unbounded energy

A release

A redemption

An opening

Hope abounds

For within the moment

Is the intention set

To sit still

And so within the stillness

Within this quiet moment

This silent interlude

Can the bridge be crossed

And the connections made

To the inner self

The true self

Open and receptive

Without judgment

Clearing the pathway

To connect

To communicate

To bend

With all that you know

With all that you believe

With all that you trust

Trust what you believe

Believe what you know

Know what you trust

Everything is connected
The knowing, the trusting, the believing
They go together
They are cornerstones
And serve as a solid foundation
A strong base
Securing a life of fulfillment
And contentment
Trust is the anchor
Trust is the key
Trust is what you believe
Trust what you know

Trust what you believe
Believe what you know
Know what you trust
Everything is connected

TO BE TRUE

Be true to yourself
True to your core
For it is the essence
Of who you are
Truth is within you
You are beholden
To the truth
It is the way
It is the path
It is your destiny
To be true
Is to be you
You are the truth
You are the way
Follow your truth
Feel what you feel
Know what you know
Be open
Be receptive
Be aware
To all that is within
You house the truth
It is within reach
For you to access
For you to explore
For you to question
The truth resides within you
Waiting to be known

To be shared
To be lived
To live fully
Is to trust fully
That life will unfold
And you will know
All you need to know
And you will learn
All you need to learn
By being true to yourself

You are beholden
To the truth
It is the way
It is the path
It is your destiny
To be true
Is to be you

LETTING GO

Take a deep breath
Inhale the energy
Feel the movement
Feel the flow
Feel the rhythm
Of the breath
Exhale the excess
That is no longer required
Inhale the life force
Breathe in the air
Feel the breath
Feel the path
Feel the way
Slow the rhythm
Slow the breath
Breathing deeply
Breathing slowly
Breathing fully
Into your inner self
Sustaining you
Nurturing you
Breathe out
Releasing the tensions
Releasing the stress
Letting go
Making room for
The next breath
For the wholeness

For the energy
Breathe
In and out
Breathe
In and out
For it is the breath
That will guide you
For it is the breath
That will sustain you
For it is the breath
That will lead you
To your inner self

THE BIRD

The wings of the bird
Enable the bird to fly
To soar to new heights
To fly to new destinations
In search of warm weather
Instinctively the bird flies
To the place
With the conditions
Right for the bird
To be able to survive
And to continue to soar
On the journey
Of being a bird
You, too, have the means to soar
To new heights
And new places
Each person has the capacity
To reach new levels
By going within
To access that which is instinctual
The natural course
Will be one of growth
And development
There is a reservoir of energy
Within each of you
Waiting to be tapped
Waiting to be used
Only you can access

The source of your power
The source of your energy
The source of your being
For each individual
Has their own reservoir
You need to go within
To generate the flow
To turn the switch
To find your power
For within you
Is unlimited energy
That will sustain you
And enable you to soar
Along the path
And on the journey
That is your life
The source of energy
Is readily available
Waiting to be activated
So as the wings of the bird
Are always ready to take flight
So, too, is your source of energy
Always ready to take you
Where you choose to go

There is a reservoir of energy
Within each of you
Waiting to be tapped

BIRTHDAY MEMORY

Twenty years of missed birthdays

Twenty years

Of missed joys

Of missed passions

Of loving

Of living

In this plane

Twenty years have passed

Missing you

Feeling you

Here but not here

Gone but not gone

Around but not around

Close yet so far

Feeling your presence

Yet missing you

In the present

So near

Yet so far

At peace

Yet a piece of you

Is missing

For us left behind

Here, there, everywhere

A world away

Yet within the world

Always in our hearts

Always a part of us

Never to be forgotten
Never to be lost
For you live on
In our memories
In our hearts
In our minds
In our souls
You are a part of us
We carry you within
Always held dearly
Always held closely
Always with love
The remembrances of days
Gone by
Of sharing
Of living
Of laughing
Of loving
An eternity ago
But here for all eternity
You live on
Through us
For we remember
The smile on your face
The twinkle in your eyes
The joy you shared
The love you spread
The friendships you formed
The children you held closely
And nurtured and loved
The bonds you formed

Never to be forgotten
Always to be cherished
Always to be remembered
Always is forever
We remember you forever
And carry you
In our hearts
In our minds
In our souls
You are a part of us
That is forever entrenched
A bond never to be broken
A chain
A link
Connecting us
For all eternity
Until we meet again
In love
In friendship
In joy
In healing
We are united
We are together
We are one
In spirit
In mind
In unity
Together as one

LEARNING PATH

The lessons of life
Unfold gradually
Minute by minute
Hour by hour
Day by day
Life is a series of experiences
And out of these experiences
Come the lessons to be learned
There is no clear order
There is no time frame
There is no beginning
And there is no end
It is a continuum
This learning path
Is different for each person
And each person
Takes the lessons
In the way
That is right for the individual
Some people get the lessons
Effortlessly and with ease
Yet for other people
The lessons require effort
And need to be repeated
Before they can be integrated
Before they can be inhaled
And become part of the person
And a piece of their understanding

For there is no right way
And there is no wrong way
To absorb the lessons
Leading to understanding
Growth and tolerance
Certain lessons may come easily
Yet others will be harder to fathom
And will be met with resistance
So each person
Will travel their path
And encounter their lessons
As they journey along
Some lessons will be absorbed
And become part of the person
And just as their breath
Sustains them
So too will the lessons
Sustain them
And lead to growth

Life is a series of experiences
And out of these experiences
Come the lessons to be learned

UNDERSTANDING

The path to understanding
Is haphazard
It is not a straight line
But meanders
Along the path
Destined for you
At times there will be
Moments of clarity
Moments of awakening
Moments of enlightenment
Yet at times there will be
Fear
Panic
Questioning
They are all part
Of the cycle
Of growth
Of renewal
Of understanding
There is no clear doctrine
Or manifesto
There is only the path
You have chosen to take
Your path will yield
The answers to your questions
Your path is your path
To travel
To explore

And to acknowledge

And to accept

The path that is yours

For each being

Travels their own path

Has their own purpose

To fulfill

To complete

To understand

Sometimes the answers

Are difficult to discern

And comprehend

Yet they all have meaning

Affecting your path

As you travel

Along the path

To understanding

Stay open

Stay centered

Stay with your breath

Let the possibilities in

Let the light in

Be in the present

Be in the moment

Be who you are

For that is what

You are meant to be

FEEL WHAT YOU BELIEVE

Believe that all is possible
Believe what you believe
For belief
Is the foundation
The building block
The fundamental core
For transformation
To occur
First there is belief
That what you believe
Is possible
Feel what you believe
Experience what you believe
Know what you believe
For to believe
Is to be Alive
Believing is knowing
Believing is understanding
It is the core of you
It is your essence
It is you
It is me
It is one
It is possible

THE FLOWER

Feel your heart
Feel your soul
Feel the feelings
That are unfolding
The flower bud
Gently opens
In all her glory
Radiating in the sunshine
Glowing in the day
The petals aligned
Gently swaying in the breeze
The flower grows
And flowers
In harmony with the elements
So, too, are you in harmony
In accord
In alignment
With all the loving gifts
The universe bestows on you
You are ready
To open to new horizons
As your heart opens
And is filled with love
There is a knowing
There is a stirring
There is a gentle unfolding
Of knowing
Of believing

Of recognizing
That all is as it should be
You will not question
Your heart knows
You are in this moment
Of true splendor
When all feels right
And you know the answers
The time is sacred
As you savor the moment
As you live in the present
Love has no boundaries
Love has no limits
Love is open
And not confined
Love is a knowing
Deep in the core
Love is a force
Touching your essence
Awakening your being
Love encompasses all
Love flows
Love is a reawakening
An affirmation
It resounds within
Opening the heart
Opening the soul
Love is eternal

FEEL THE LIGHT

The echoes of the past
Resound in the present
Listen in the quiet
Listen in the solitude
Listen in the silence
Feel the vibrations
Feel the energy
Feel the light
Entering your being
And infusing you with light
With energy
With essence
With familiarity
Knowing that all is
As it should be
And that you
Know the answers
To the questions
You have asked
The end is not the beginning
And the beginning is not the end
It is a continuum
A circle
An ever evolving sphere
That goes on and on
Transcending all levels
Transcending all space
Transcending all time
To bring you to the present

To this sacred moment
When all is as it is
Meant to be
We are here to guide you
We are here to support you
We are here to nurture you
As you travel along your path
You are surrounded by light
By love
By energy
And in the stillness
You listen
And in the quiet
You hear
And in the solitude
You know
From the depth
Of your heart
You know
All that you need
To know

The end is not the beginning
And the beginning is not the end
It is a continuum
A circle
An ever evolving sphere
That goes on and on

THE GIFT

The beautifully wrapped present
Adorned with ribbons
And colorful bows
Waiting to be opened
Waiting to be experienced
Waiting to be cherished
The anticipation
The excitement
The curiosity
To know the present
To feel the present
To claim the present
For the gift
Is in the present
And the present
Is in the gift
Of being in the moment
Of opening up
Of unwrapping the layers
And exposing the core
The essence
Of what lies within
The present
The gift is a metaphor
For this present moment
For you to be

GO WITH THE FLOW

Remember it all begins

With self-love

Nurturing

Caring

Listening

To the songs from within

Going into the silence

Going into the quiet

Going into the solitude

Accessing your reservoir

Of peace

Of harmony

Of inner contentment

Go with the breath

Go with the flow

Go with the energy

Available to you

At all times

Enabling you to live

The life

You are meant to live

A NEW DAY

A new day has dawned
Heralding in light
And the promise
Of new beginnings
Each day
Starts afresh
And anew
Yesterday has passed
And with it the memories
Of days gone by
Of the life you have lived
To this juncture
Of the choices you have made
Of the roads you have travelled
All culminating
And bringing you
To this moment in time
For it is in this present moment
That you are born
And reborn
Every day
Giving you the opportunity
For rebirth
For planting new seeds
For growing
As you were meant to grow
The choices you make
In the present

Are the foundation
Upon which you
Build your tomorrows
Live each day
Learn each day
Explore each day
Love each day
For it is a gift
To be in the present
To be in this moment
To be in this time
For today
Is always a new beginning
A time of hope
A time of being
A time to be
To be in this time
To be in this moment
To be in the present
Is the greatest gift
Of all time

For today
Is always a new beginning
A time of hope
A time of being
A time to be

EACH DAY IS A NEW ADVENTURE

The day has dawned
A fresh beginning
A time to start anew
Yesterday has passed
And the past is behind
A reflection
A mirror
A photographic snapshot
Of time well spent
Today starts anew
A blank canvas
An empty slate
A clean page
Waiting to be filled
With possibilities
With potential
Each day is a new adventure
You embark on
As you arise
And set your compass
For the way you will travel
And how you will proceed
There is no map
There are no clear guidelines
The journey you take
Begins with the first step
From whence progression will happen
Taking the step
Moves you in the direction

You will travel
Sometimes the journey
Will be arduous
The directions will not be clear
There will be obstacles
There will be road blocks
There will be detours
There will be setbacks
And at times the journey
And the road ahead
Will forge crystal clear
And you will flow
Effortlessly
Easily
Along the path
You travel
As a bird
Soars in the sky
Riding in the currents
Of the wind
Not fighting
Not resisting
Not opposing
The natural flow
But gliding
With the wind
In the elements
Being one with nature
Being one with the universe
Being one
Being

THE WHISPER OF YOUR SOUL

The seasons come
And the seasons go
A time for growing
And a time to let go
A time for breathing
And a time for releasing
The winter is a time
To seek shelter
From the harsh elements
A time to go within
To the sanctuary
That offers solace
Through the storm
A time to retreat
A time to reflect
A time to rebuild
For the storm shall pass
And the cold, icy days
Will be replaced
By the promise of spring
A time to grow
A time to renew
A time to sprout
But now it is time
To seek refuge
To go within the silence
To access your inner self
To listen to your spirit

To feel your heart
To hear the whisper of your soul
To listen to the voice within
To find the strength
To keep moving forward
Slowly, slowly, slowly
No rush to the finish line
For the journey
Is one of many steps
And many lessons
To be learned along the way
Some experiences
Taking your breath away
Seeming so perfect in the moment
But everything is fleeting
And there will be transitions
And hardships
To counter the perfection
And to balance the scales
Life is a flow of experiences
Of moments and times
Of joy and sorrow
Of peace and strife
Of harmony and discord
Of living and dying
Each moment unfolding into the next
The past leading to the present
As the present folds into the future
The rhythmic unfolding of the moments
Living in the present
Breathing in the essence

Feeling the feelings
Of the moment
Knowing that each moment
Is a transition to the next
The good times shall pass
The bad times shall pass
For there is always flow
As the universe
Seeks to balance the scales
Enjoying the good
Enduring the bad
Learning and growing
Reflecting and rebuilding
Living moment by moment
Living hour by hour
Living day by day
Staying in the moment
Being in the present
Being in the flow

But now it is time
To seek refuge
To go within the silence
To access your inner self
To listen to your spirit
To feel your heart
To hear the whisper of your soul

6840720R00130

Made in the USA
San Bernardino, CA
16 December 2013